A JOURNEY WITHIN

A JOURNEY WITHIN
OLIVIA FRASER

Grosvenor Gallery

CONTENTS

A Journey Within

My encounter with India has been like a journey, reflected in what I paint and how I paint. Starting off as a physical journey when I was twenty-three and free from responsibilities, where I would travel and sketch from life, this journey has transformed into a metaphysical one travelling inwards, in tandem with the onset of family life and perhaps a deeper, longer engagement with the country, where I have attempted to dive into the language, philosophy and poetic, artistic and spiritual traditions of India.

I first came to India in 1989 clasping a newly published book called *The Passionate Quest*. It was a glossy, hardback coffee-table book written by Mildred Archer and Toby Falk about the art and adventures of my Scottish kinsmen, James and William Fraser, in India from 1801 to 1835.

James Baillie Fraser was a landscape artist who, during the early years of the nineteenth century, painted a hugely popular series of engravings and lithographs of the Himalayas and cityscapes of Calcutta, now found in every club and hotel across India. His brother, William, was the british resident representing the East India Company in Delhi.

This was during the period of the White Mughals, when the East India Company employees living in India had assimilated themselves into Indian culture, learning the languages, dressing in local costume, eating local food and taking on Indian wives. William Fraser was one of the most flamboyant White Mughals – a patron and friend of the sufis, scholars and poets of Delhi and father of 'more children than the King of Persia'. Perhaps the most interesting aspect of this was the extraordinary watercolours which James and he commissioned from Delhi artists. These paintings formed what has become the famous 'Fraser Album' – perhaps the supreme masterpiece of late Mughal and Company School Painting, portraying the different types of people in Delhi and their jobs, crafts and castes, all against stark white backgrounds. This hybrid form of painting where Indian artists created something that mixed techniques and ideas from the East and West has greatly influenced me and was the starting point for all my work.

Arriving in Delhi fresh from art school in 1989, I started using the travel-friendly medium of watercolour and set about painting the people I encountered on my travels around India, inspired by the depictions in the 'Fraser Album'.

I also painted architectural elevations, such as the monuments of Delhi and elsewhere as I led a very itinerant life.

At that time, I visited the National Museum in Delhi and discovered Indian miniature painting. I was thrilled by the gem-like colours, the detailed brushwork, the iterative patterning and the burnished surfaces. But I was also attracted to the confidence of the iconography, the symbolism and the meanings behind the use of colour, shape and infinitely fine line, and this too inspired my paintings over the next decade or so.

It wasn't until 2005 when, on returning to Delhi with my young family, I was determined to actually master these traditional techniques. I apprenticed myself to a miniature painting workshop in Jaipur. I would spend hours watching and listening to the master painter, Ajay Sharma, as he managed to make his studio materials a microcosm of the world outside, channeling it into his work and relating it to how he used a certain sap from a particular tree outside his front door or a chalk white (khariya) from the cliffs around Jaipur, local flower petals soaked and distilled for their colour or soot from his oil lamp to make the black khajal with – excellent for fine line work. Ajay, like many of the Jaipuri miniature painters, was from a family who worked in the gem industry; the gemstone and painting worlds being closely connected as semi-precious stones are used for painting. Ajay

taught me about grinding and mixing pigments to their correct consistency. I learnt how to make the wasli, binding the thin handmade paper together, priming it and burnishing it with an agate stone. What I enjoyed most was using the single-haired squirrel brushes. These have a natural spring and curve at the tip which, together with the almost meditational concentration required for this genre, facilitates the drawing of perfect miniature circles and spirals.

When I came across Srinathji paintings from the Nathdwara tradition near Udaipur, I became fascinated by the philosophy and the spiritual aspect underpinning this painting tradition: the sacred geometry, structure, colour, symbolism, the fact that as with Byzantine icons, these artworks were objects of worship and devotion.

A piece of serendipity led me to discover an art studio in Delhi where giant pichwais (temple backdrops for icons of Krishna in his child-like eighth incarnation as Srinathji) on linen were being created. Sitting on the floor with the other studio craftsmen, all playing their part in making the vast pichwai, I learned through a process of osmosis. I became obsessed by the rigour of the traditional Indian miniature painting process; particularly this Nathdwara-inspired sacred art. It involved a different way of seeing – there was only one way to paint a banana leaf; you didn't go out and sketch from life, so much as reach for its essence. It was an internal form of perception rather than an external one – about knowing and seeing rather than the more Western gaze of estimating and looking. Pichwais are bound by strict iconographic rules, with sacred geometry and proportion integral to the symbolic meaning and structure of the whole. So Srinathji's features are based on the geometry and proportion of the original svarupa, or deity, housed in the shrine at Nathdwara.

Pichwais and miniature painting use the same techniques and have the same studio practice, so I would sit beside these artists in the studio painting my own Nathdwara-inspired artwork. Initially I opreated on a miniature scale, but after a few years, I too started working on a pichwai scale – in feet rather than in inches.

In 2008, I went to the US to see a show put on by the Freer Sackler called 'Garden and Cosmos'. There I saw Maharaja Man Singh's Jodhpuri paintings from the early nineteenth century inspired by the Nath yogic tradition. A yoga practitioner myself, I felt I was witnessing something profoundly relevant and eternal. Themes inspired by the scriptures have been used throughout art history, but this was a particularly Indian vision painted with an Indian art vocabulary which seemed to have universal and contemporary resonance. The monumental fields of colour making up the cosmic oceans with their esoteric concepts and dream-like intensity pre-empted twentieth-century artists like Rothco, Howard Hodgkin and Sol Le Witt.

I feel there is a natural affinity between a traditional Indian artistic aesthetic, whether it be Tantric art or miniature painting, and Western ideas of Minimalism, Op art and Geometric Abstraction. All explore essence, sensation and perception. I have sought to combine these perspectives by focusing in on the iterative, pairing it down to the minimal and ultimately striving to reach for an essence while also pursuing the idea of movement, which is innate in the texts and practices of yoga.

I have a deep and abiding interest in yoga and my practice of it. With yoga's current global popularity as a fitness regime and a means towards a perfect body, it's easy to forget its ancient historical roots in India which reveal it to have a far more wide-ranging spiritual and philosophical practice and meaning.

The word 'yoga' comes from the Sanskrit term meaning 'union' and is etymologically linked to the English word 'yoke'. It is about connecting the mind, body and soul and harnessing the senses in an everflowing movement towards liberation, or the absolute, which in yogic philosophy lies as much within the body as without. One of the pathways to achieving this is meditation, and within that, the practice of visualization using images from landscape, in particular lotuses, and linking them with the metaphysical. This is partly to shut out everyday thoughts and emotions, but also partly as an aid in itself to propelling one's inner focus forward and upwards. This results in a clarity and peace far removed from the distractions and stresses of the everyday world.

In Indian art, especially in the Jain and Tantric traditions from Rajasthan and Gujarat, there is a tradition of assisting yoga practitioners to achieve this by providing what are in effect visual roadmaps to spiritual enlightenment. These take many different forms, ranging from mandalas and yantras, which are believed to store and generate positive energies, to maps of the subtle body, which represent the idea of the body as a microcosm of the universe. Inspired by this, I have painted a variety of spiritual roadmaps where there is a visual – almost narrative – development of the pathway towards enlightenment, using the lotus within as the driving force and moving from ideas associated with gross meditation to the more profound, subtle and luminous meditation, and ultimately to creation.

I've drawn on tradition in a variety of ways, many of which are linked to the symbol of the lotus as the archetypal icon of yoga, used as a tool for visualization given its association with perfection, renunciation and spiritual growth. In different paintings I pull the lotus apart, deconstructing it, iterating it, expanding and contracting it, unravelling it, isolating it into icons both large and small, exploring its association with colour and with the senses, its connection to the ground and the cosmos, to other metaphorical poetic icons like the bee and to Indian philosophy and poetry. I am now concerned with inner landscapes rather than external ones, so the majority of my works over the last few years are painted or enclosed within a square format, reflecting the idea of a mandala with its associations of energized space and acute meditation.

I'm using the materials, techniques and vocabulary I learnt in the traditional Indian miniature painting studio. This is a slow art form. Everything is hand-made from materials I don't have to go far to find in the world around me: whether it is my handmade jute wasli paper, the kharia or chalk white from the cliffs around Jaipur, nuts and sap from local trees, soot black from oil lamps or semi-precious stones like malachite or lapis garnered as off-cuts from the gemstone markets in Jaipur. I create imagery of the landscape using elements from the landscape, crushed, ground, mixed and polished. Surfaces are flat but the process is highly tactile and textural.

In an ever accelerating world hell-bent on accentuating our differences, I feel this slow art form and my subject matter, probing a vision or journey within, is a wonderful antidote, emphasizing as it does the importance of slowing down, connecting and being present in the moment.

OLIVIA FRASER

Olivia's Subtle World

This world around us: one can see it through the doorway of the eyes (chakshu-dvaara); but it is through the mind alone (mano-dvaara) that it can be known.
– old Sanskrit saying

I am convinced that somehow, somewhere, at some point of time, Olivia Fraser heard a chatak: that all but inaudible sound, soft and warm, that – at least in the imagination of Urdu poets – a bud makes at the precise moment of opening its petals. There is a wonderful verse that the poet Josh Malihabadi once wrote: 'itna maanoos hoon fitrat sey kali jab chataki / jhuk key mainey yeh kahaa, "mujh sey kuchh irshaad kiya?"'(So close am I to Nature that when the bud opened and made that chatak sound, I bent my head low and asked, 'was it me that you were speaking to?') Olivia, I believe, could have written that verse if only she knew enough Urdu. For such is the level of subtleties that she also 'hears' and weaves into her work.

There is something even in the early work of her old Scottish forebear, James Baillie Fraser's keen eye: putting 'an impression down with precision'. One cannot miss in those early watercolours of hers the precise moment of light about to depart from a carved pillar, an old man trying hard to focus on the newspaper in his trembling hands, a young girl

struggling to keep the child on her hip from slipping down, and the like. But there is so much more to it: a sense of deep engagement, a desire to understand what is behind all that one sees, a refusal to accept appearances for what they are. The great nineteenth-century Urdu poet, Mirza Ghalib, echoing ancient Indian thought, had cautioned himself, and us all, including her of course, when he wrote: 'hasti key mat fareb mein aa jaaiyo Asad! / aalam tamaam halqa-e daam-e khayaal hai' (Be not deceived by all that is around you, friend! For all that you see is but one loop in the vast net of imagination).

Indian painters of the past had ways of seeing which were sometimes all their own. This Olivia could sense when she entered their world at some point of time: abstract thoughts captured in seemingly simple visuals; ideas dug out from the roots of the past, taken in hand and then thrown clear beyond the reach of time; spaces that peered through the interstices of the mind at one moment and then, in the next, enlarged, expanded, as if to reach the very farthest end possible. This magical world, visible to all those who 'do not refuse to see with the transfiguring eyes of love', in Coomaraswamy's ringing words, seems to have opened itself up to Olivia slowly. She worked under master painters nurtured in the tradition and kept absorbing whatever she could see and hear, even as she sat on the floor grinding pigments, feeling the texture of paper with her bare hands, trimming hair taken from squirrels' tails and binding them together to fashion a brush. There were things here that were not easy to comprehend for one steeped in Western ways and thought; connections between art and life not easy to make. But gradually things started falling into place for Olivia, it would seem. Some things were easy, others not necessarily so. But when themes and motifs that early Indian painting is suffused with kept appearing again and again before her eyes, getting to explore them, engage and struggle with them must have seemed both challenging and uplifting. Take, for example, the case of the lotus, that unspeakably beautiful, layered flower which Olivia has made her own, so to speak. There they are – lotuses – as buds; as calyxes; as full-blown flowers; with long stalks or without them; bearing quivering, winking drops of water, spreading their petals out as if inviting the gods to perch on them so as to 'distance' them from the earth which belongs to mere mortals. There is a whole range of them that occur in Indian texts and thought; in fact there are at least twenty-four words for lotus that ancient lexicons give. The most commonly used words might be 'padma', 'kamala' or 'pankaj' – the last often serving as a symbol for personal purity, for it means 'that which grows in muddy waters (but in itself stays unsullied)'. But there are others: 'nalin', 'aravinda', 'utpala', 'sarasija', 'saugandhika', 'kalhara', 'kuvalya', for instance. There are however no exact synonyms; thus, 'rajiva' is that which is 'streaked' or 'striped'; 'pundarika' is 'that which bears a sacred mark', 'raktotapala' is that

which contains a burst of red colour, 'sitambhoja' is all 'white and bountiful', and so on. Olivia might not have had an intimate knowledge of each variety or type of lotus, but when they appear in her paintings – and they so often do – one can see that they differ ever so subtly, one from the other. They turn gold at some golden moment and sprout tips of brilliant red at another; tower tall or shed their stems at will. As they grow, they smile and sway together even as each of them carries around itself its own aura of auspiciousness.

Her interests expanding with time, this sense of auspiciousness, an awareness of sacred spaces and of ritual concerns, can be seen seeping and spreading everywhere in Olivia's work. And one finds her conversing, as it were, with adoring members of the magical circle that moves with Krishna at its still centre. Her engagement with pichhwais – those painted sacred textiles that celebrate the icon of lotus-eyed Krishna as installed in the great shrine of Nathdwara in Rajasthan – and all that one sees in them, turns deep. Tilak marks on the forehead, sacred footprints, gaily decorated cows (Krishna's cows), clusters of moons, heaps of petals almost spiralling out of control – this is the world one sees scrolling down in front of our eyes. Surely, there is an interest in the graphics of it all, but it goes far beyond that, for there are levels of significance that lie buried in them. They are reminders; hints of things experienced but not seen; keys to a magical world. When one sees just a forehead and a pair of large, stylized eyes, one looks again, for the tilak mark on the forehead descends like a rapier from the top, as if to cut through layers of unknowing, and in the eyes are pupils in which Krishna's face is reflected. 'Baso morey nainan mein Nandlal!' the great sixteenth-century saint-poet Mirabai had pleaded once: 'Come Krishna, Nanda's son; make my eyes your home.' Is this what was in Olivia's mind, one is entitled to wonder.

There is a whole range of paintings in which Krishna's turbaned head – in his stylized Srinathji form at Nathdwara: dark like the monsoon cloud, large and gently lowered eyes, broad forehead, studded diamond glistening in a tiny pit in the chin – becomes the centre of the painting and things happen, or revolve as it were, around it. Peacocks flutter or dance about, stylized clouds peer down, cows gaze with love in their eyes, fragrant flowers bloom; at one point aspects of the same face form a circle around the central surround as if rotating. I find myself moving toward poetry while speaking of Olivia's work, but then that is what her works do: evoke memories, seek parallels, travel to other realms. This image of hers reminds me of the words of the poet Seemaab Akbarabadi: 'rafta rafta ho gaye gardish mein jalway sainkadon / dil mera Seemaab ik aaina-khana ho gaya' (A hundred images of that beloved face began whirling around me suddenly; it is as if my heart had turned into a hall of mirrors).

As time passes, Olivia seems to dive deeper and deeper into ancient Indian thought, to come up with new, dew-drop-fresh images. She sets out in search of seven oceans and seven continents; invents symbols for the five elements and then reverses them to suggest dissolution; piles of footprints are arranged in the shape of a pyramid to suggest pilgrimage up to a mountain top; petals seemingly scattered on a surface appear to be on the point of turning into a mandala. Surely not everything in Oliva's work makes references to yoga or yogic practices, nor is everything related to ritual practices. There is playfulness in the work, too, and abstractions are tossed about. One might see a herd of overlapping cows as having walked out of Krishna's Vrindavana, but similarly overlapping herds of camels or goats are simply crisp graphics. There are visual surprises that she springs at the same time: at the heart of a surround of perfect circles, each featuring a limned lotus, one might find another circle at the centre in which there is an intense blue lotus with Krishna eyes; the hosts of humming insects moving in narrowing circles towards the centre in the 'Bhramari' group bear the aspect of lotuses themselves at first. There is a quiet, understated sense of joy in all this.

Given the rate at which Olivia is moving, one might begin to speculate on what is going to come next. Fire and its seven tongues? Ritual yajnashalas with abstract renderings of the nine planets? Or is it going to be a padmabandha: words of a verse artfully arranged in the form of a lotus? Who knows?

B . N . G O S W A M Y

KRISHNA'S GARDEN

Olivia Fraser: A Passionate Quest

Fraser's paintings reveal an intimate knowledge of the miniature practice, gained from her years of apprenticeship with the ustad Ajay Sharma in Jaipur. Regular participation in the workshop led Fraser to experience the rigorous training required to master the technique.

After seven years of apprenticeship, Fraser's technique is impeccable. Her drawing is delicate, her handling of the brush is sensitive, her colours have the density imbued by steady layering of thin veils of the stone pigments. Certain images in this exhibition bear witness to her former practice as a watercolour artist and figurative illustrator. Her terrain here is quite simply the cosmos: where the sacred creation narrative of the Rigveda is illuminated by lotuses inspiring fertility, where trees transpire towards mountains that embrace them in a protective mould. However, the majority of her forms are abstract and geometric. Horizontals hover, triangles interact, circles circumambulate and rectangles frame frames moving inwards as if to protect the deity in the mandala.

Inspiration for Fraser's recent work has come from the revelation of monumental manuscript paintings rediscovered in Marwar. These pieces reveal an extraordinary dimension of Rajput court art. Their distinctive fusion of Jodhpur–Marwar school painting allies devotional Nath iconography with minimalist abstraction. This curious shift came in the late nineteenth century with the sectarian order Nath Sampraday, a sect that since the twelfth century had initiated the hatha yoga practices inspired by earlier Tantric rituals and imagery.

Another source of inspiration for Fraser has been the Nathdwara pichwai painting from Mewar. Nathdwara painting is embedded in the Pushti Marga (Path of Grace), a bhakti sect founded by Vallabhacharya and followed by the devotees of the Vaishnava ritual. Patronage lay in the Gujarati mercantile community where the goswamis, in their role as poets, philosophers and aesthetes, introduced chitra-seva, the worship of the painted icon, thus nurturing the priestly tradition of art patronage into the domain of secular connoisseurship, now crucial to contemporary Indian culture. This evolved by way of mass production of its primary icon: Krishna in his childlike incarnation as Srinathji.

In 2006, Fraser was invited to join the studio of the specialist in pichwai painting, Desmond Lazaro, who had studied under the renowned Bannuji from Jaipur. 'Pichwais were bound by strict iconographic rules, with sacred geometry and proportion integral to the symbolic meaning and structure of the whole. I loved the rigour and exuberance in this style with its significant sacred underpinning ... I was keen to discover the origin of the sacred shapes, structure, colour and form as this all became relevant to my own practice as an artist looking into the sacred Hindu tradition.' Scarcely anything was known about the monumental miniatures of Jodhpur until the rigorous scholarship of Debra Diamond. Her curatorial acuity resulted in the wondrous exhibition 'Garden and Cosmos' which revealed the extraordinary scale and scope of Jodhpur at the time. The Nath's teachings had already influenced Rajput art, but the extraordinary transformation was made within the Jodhpur tradition when painting shifted into a very different world during the reign of Maharajah Man Singh between 1803 and 1843. The history is occluded as if the very esotericism of the movement has drawn a veil over the facts. The Nath Siddhis were linked to Tantric orders, where experimental practices based on hatha yoga were pushed to elaborate degrees of risk and reward.

As Maha Siddhis (the perfected ones), their enlightenment would enable them not only to be gurus and fly across the cosmic stratas but their upward mobility allowed them to become soldiers, policy advisors, controllers of revenues and bankers, even speculating in real estate. This is the background which partially explains the sumptuousness of their paintings – vast in scale yet reduced in content, the intensity of their abstract colour fields is heightened with the exquisite ornamentation of gold and silver leaf. The paradox of an aesthetic richness – a sort of cool baroque – stuns the viewer into a sense of bhakti. Fascinating as it is to ponder on the sources of such an innovatory conception, its contemporary relevance may be demonstrated through the work of Olivia Fraser.

'I came to be interested in the esoteric world of Tantric art when my interest shifted from Company and Mughal painting to Hindu/Rajasthani painting … it seemed to have very ancient pre-Mughal roots, certainly in terms of shape, colour, form and iconography … In my search to really understand the roots of this world, it seemed to me that they were built on a very strong, rigorous backbone of arcane knowledge and that Tantric art could contain answers to my questions.'

The principal difference between other images informed by Tantric sadhana and the Nath paintings lies in their depictions of the absolute. In the more familiar yantras, it is an abstract, infinitely formless entity, often simply a blank space onto which the meditator projects her own inner yantra. The Sri Yantras (power diagrams) set out to reveal the underlying structure of the universe. Dynamics in yantras depict the eternal flux of opposites: active and passive, male and female. Triangles interact to unite in the nucleus or Bindu, which symbolizes the union of all opposites: subject and object, creation and destruction. Concentration on the yantra, together with the repetition of mantras, yield a focus on the immediate moment as a way to disconnect the yogin from everyday illusion and reintegrate with the void.

Although the Naths shared this vision, they added pictorial elements through portraiture and signs. For example, the self-numinous Brahman is depicted in the form of Nathji, the sublime Maha Siddhi based on the immortal ascetic Jallandharnath. Squatting gracefully on cosmic seas of golden pigment, he has the distinctive Nath Siddhi features of a curved nose profile, neatly pageboy dreadlocks and red-tinged almond eyes.

Fraser's recent work shows an appreciation of such figurative aspects. In pieces such as 'I See Him Now' and 'Seven Oceans, Seven Continents' she plays with the Srinathji Krishna icon, duly traced in indigo pigment on a yellow ground, either full-faced and cocky with his tilted Mount Meru hat or gradually stripped of features to become a mask-like cut-out frieze, where a single hand or foot can replace the image. Her staging of the Srinathji icon has a hint of the vivacity which imbued her earlier illustrations of everyday life in India. It is particularly relevant to signal here that her forebears were the celebrated Fraser brothers, William and James Baillie Fraser, who actually commissioned watercolours from local Indian artists to make the 'Fraser Album'.

The specific elements that Fraser has adopted in her recent works are the reductive, minimalist forms. Rectangles and strips present flat fields of vibrating colour condensed into finely wrought pattern work. These recycle familiar motifs for cosmic waters, such as the basket weave pattern, first seen in Ajanta frescoes and later in Pahari miniatures. Fraser's 'Genesis' triptych aligns three squares, of which two encase a precious flame-patterned cosmic eggs floating in ethereal space or wild waters; gem-like, they fuse the sacred Siva and the profane Faberge. Writing on this work, Fraser cites the lines, 'In the beginning arose the Cosmic Embryo …' and adds, 'I came to painting the cosmic egg series when reading the Rigveda. Having painted the one with the swirling waters, I then saw Manaku's image: a huge golden egg in swirling waters, so like mine but minus my lines of fire.' Other pieces like 'The Churning Ocean' seem to knit together layers of 'scalloped whorls', producing a similar effect to the scroll cloud work found in Tibetan thangka paintings, inspired by Mongolian and Chinese landscape imagery. Fraser's hues – subtle greys and rosy pinks, mellow yellows and malachite greens – all shimmer luminosity. One 'Shiv Shakti' triptych presents two parallel crimson and cream squares, enclosing male and female triangles. Gender is spelt out through the voluptuous yellow and blue lotus forms in the 'Radha Krishna' diptych. In 'Holy Mountain' we see stark angular trees under Mount Merus, stylized like ice cream cones. This is a very different piece; one with the anecdotal quality of Fraser's tender watercolours. The delicate scrollwork in 'Creation' recycles the elaborate circumferences of the mandala protecting the virtual deity.

The monumental miniatures in 'Garden and Cosmos' are at once sacred and comic. Their 'lightness of being' originates in the links between narrative and abstraction found in the ancient texts, as Fraser writes:

'When you get into the realm of the sacred, text and image are almost one, hence the written word 'Om' (amongst others) frequently being used by artists as a form of visual expression. Any research into the origins of Tantric/Hindu art can't really begin without looking at ancient scripture, so, looking at the stories and bhakti texts relating to Krishna as well, including the ninth-century poet Nammalvar's wonderful *Hymns for the Drowning*, which are sacred hymns to Krishna's principal incarnation as Vishnu, I started reading the Rigveda and the Upanishads, and was thrilled to find how rich and abstractly visual they all were. I was particularly captivated by the creation mythology with its distant echoes and its differences from sacred texts in the West.'

Fraser is clearly intrigued with an intercultural play between past and present. On coming to India in 1989, she bought a book called *The Passionate Quest* by Mildred Archer and Toby Falk that recounts the adventures of her illustrious antecedants, the Fraser Brothers, between 1801 and 1835. She is inspired by artists who have approached the 'other' or the unfamiliar with the experience of displacement, whether it be through the physical, as with Gauguin, or the imaginary, as with Henri Rousseau. Contemporary artists whom Fraser admires include Anish Kapoor, Sol Le Witt and Steven Cox – artists whose practices encompass inter-ocular perspectives.

The common sense of 'no future' amongst Western youth was described half a century ago in *Growing Up Absurd* by Paul Goodman, who saw the problem in Utopian terms: 'The spirit of modern society has not sufficiently realized itself.' If Rousseau's 'tourbillion social' of the eighteenth century became Marx's 'maelstrom' in the nineteenth century, the slaughter of the twentieth century has become the bloodbath of the twenty-first century. Current global turmoil is aptly framed within the spirit of the Kali Yuga, the contemporary dark age pithily described by Doniger as 'the losing age, the time when all bets are off'.

Texts on Kali Yuga state that the search for sense takes place within the modern experience; one seen either as a fallen condition or as a vehicle for experimental transformation.

The latter is the vision set out by the Tantric doctors in their rejection of the orthodox Brahmanic tradition and their return to the pre-Vedic cult of Shakti as the great goddess.

Fraser's minimalist visual language suggests an affinity with the Tantric imagery on a formal level, but comparison may offer analogies in metaphysical terms. Whereas Tantric symbols have a specific function as tools or aids in meditation, abstract forms in Western art are often perceived as free floating signs, even as 'illegitimate abstraction'. Yantras have a specific function to the initiated, but to the uninitiated they can be appreciated on account of their vibrant patterns, purist shapes and primary colours for their affinity with Western abstract art. Whereas yantras are via media on the void, art objects are via media in the exercise of changing perception. May this exercise have the metaphysical implications claimed by those early twentieth-century artists whose practices related to universalist concerns with the metphysical?

Artists such as Malevitch, Kandinsky and Mondrian made serious use of theosophy. Their neo-platonism declares a spiritual idealism exempt of the irony diffused in postmodernist discourse.

When Rauschenberg said he worked in the gap between art and life, Cage said there was no gap; that art lies in 'simply being ... our highest business in our daily life'. He saw art as the process of making, as Duchamp himself described the origins of art. Where yantras require contemplation from the yogini, Duchamp's work invites an active participation from the viewer to complete. Perhaps making images work through collaboration with the viewer might be compared to the Hindu ritual of darshan?

I would question the assumption whereby the spiritual in art is frequently framed by Western critics as the 'other' or of another time. There is profuse evidence that all such qualities may be found in the history of Western imagery, not only in abstraction but in representation as well. Currently in an exhibition of medieval manuscripts in the British Library, there is a miniature of a 'Diagram of Consanguinity' made in 1320, which has a mandala format containing rows of empty circles which prefigure Baldessari's paintings. So Fraser has not just been borrowing from an alien or 'other' tradition; the two traditions have long been in dialogue.

The very practice of Tantra aims at revealing the illusion of opposites: micro–macro, the sacred in the mundane. If, as according to Levi-Strauss, there needed to be a common structure to compare two creative languages, it would only be possible if a Western artist underwent Tantric initiation and found a phenomena which could be related structurally. Fraser has undergone initiation into Tantric-inspired miniature painting and the formal and metaphysical affinities in her practice integrate a comparable pattern of relationship with the spiritual. Her intense images invite a meditation on the ways of looking.

VIRGINIA WHILES
January 2012

Dance of the Peacocks
(Bagicha Ka Utsava), 2006
(OF0601)

Gopashtami
(Triptych), 2007
(OF0701)

Krishna's Garden, 2008
(OF0801)

Your Eyes, 2008
(OF0804)

Shiva, 2009
(OF0901)

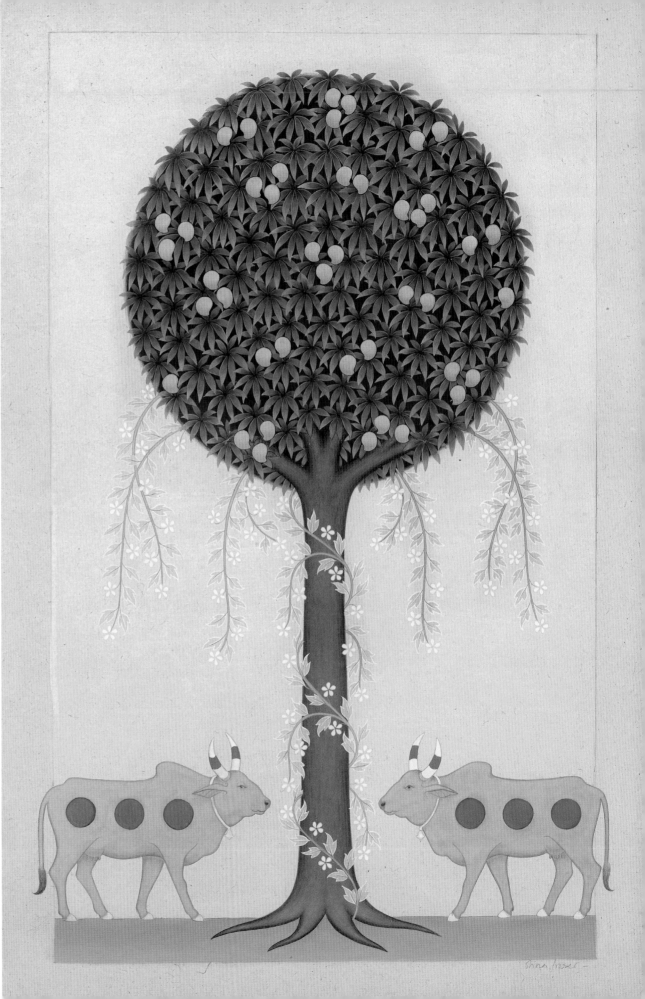

Krishna I, 2010
(OF1005)

Krishna II, 2010
(OF1006)

Krishna III, 2010   **Becoming Krishna, 2010**
(OF1007)   (OF0903)

**Seven Oceans, Seven
Continents, 2010**
(OF1001)

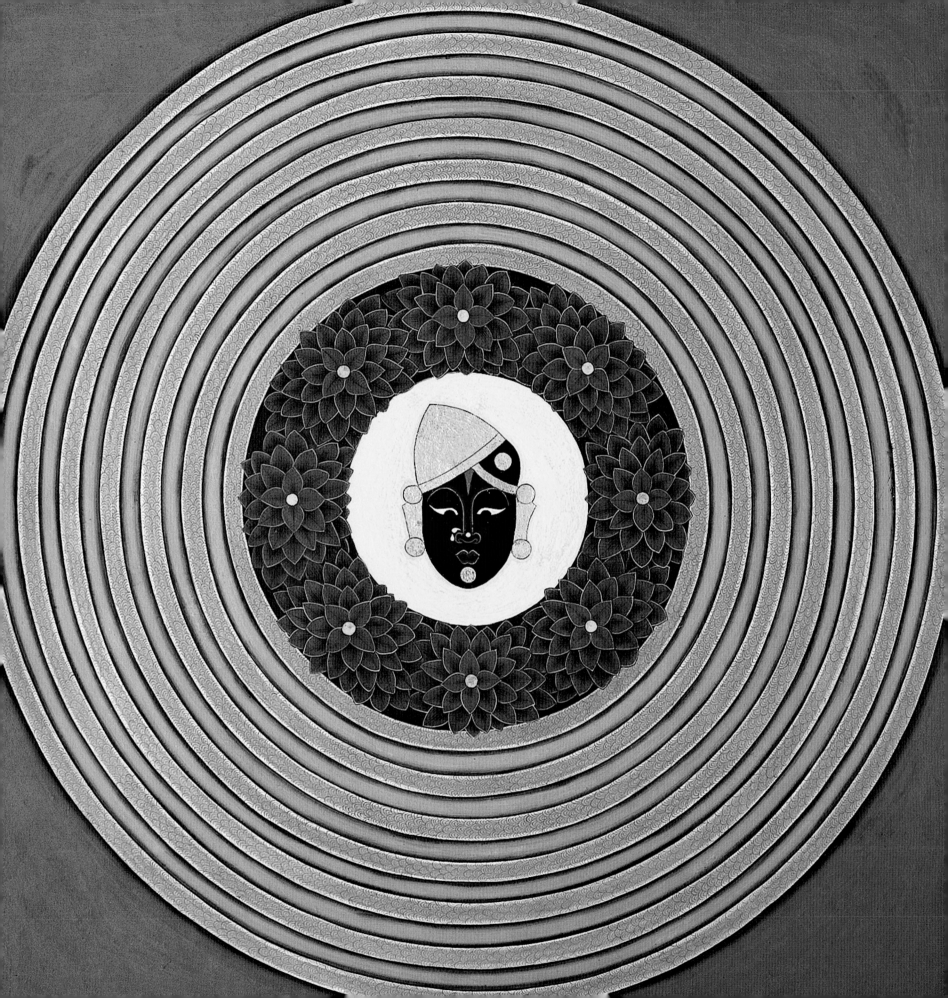

Mt Govardhan, 2010
(OF1002)

Godhuli Bela, 2011
(OF1108)

Dusk, 2012
(OF1203)

Cosmic Body, 2010
(OF1113)

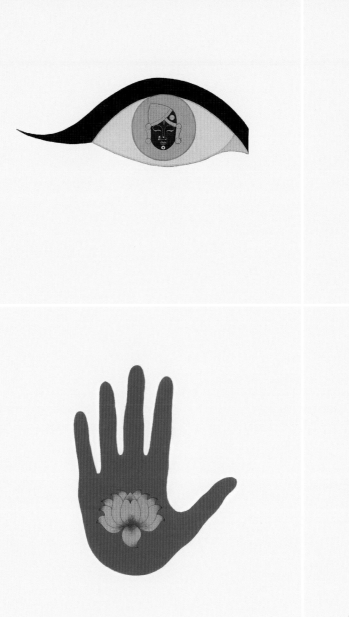

I See Him Now, 2011
(OF1105)

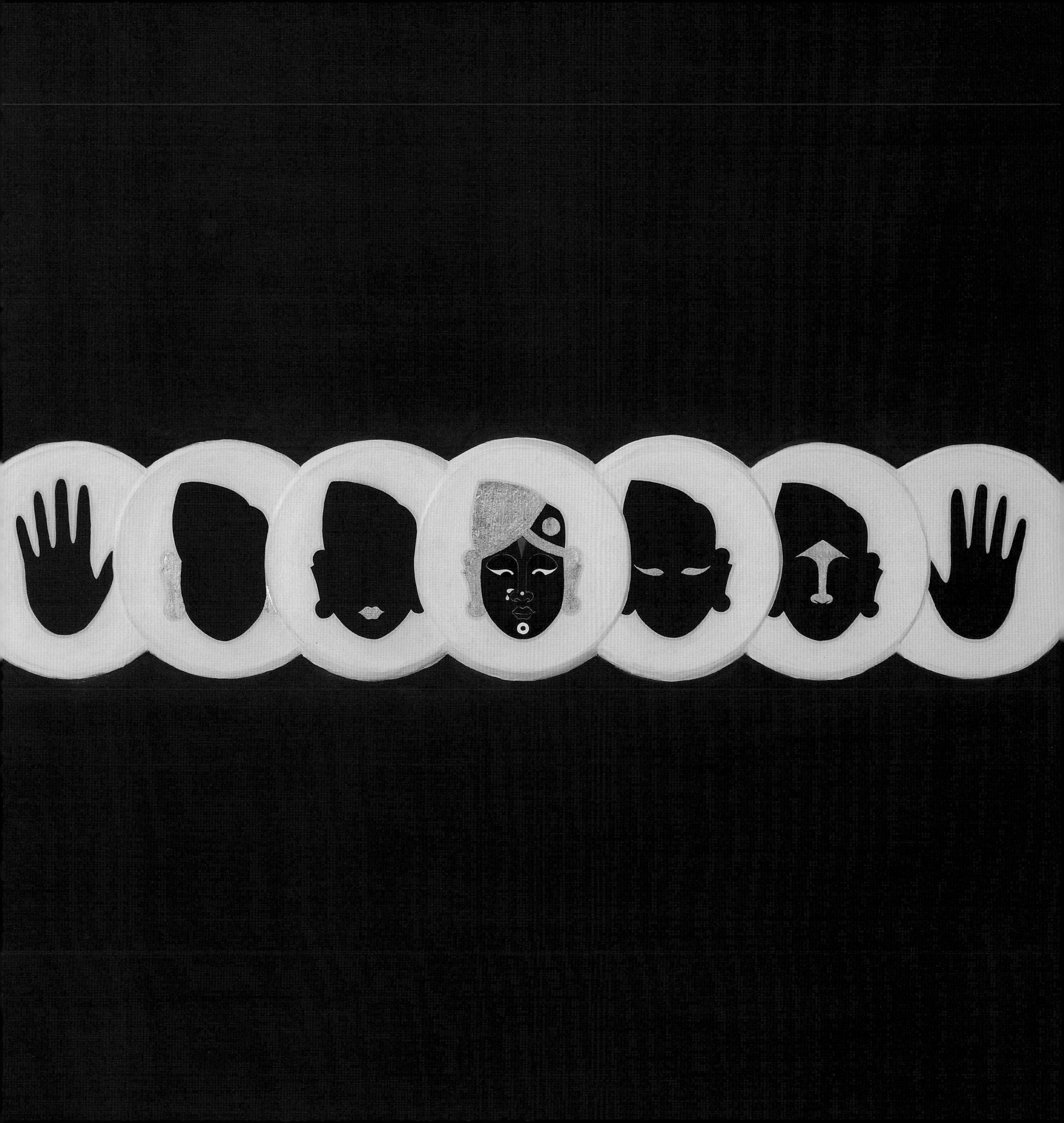

Shiv Shakti (Triptych), 2011
(OF1106)

(preceding spread)

Radha Krishna, 2011
(OF1104)

The Blue Lotus, 2012
(OF1208)

Rasa Lila, 2013
(OF1306)

SACRED
LANDSCAPE

A Sacred Garden

Olivia Fraser applies pigment on paper with a clarity and intent that instinctually pleases the eye. Strong colour, evenly applied and satisfyingly thick, remains firmly within the boundaries of clearly delineated, often repeating forms spread over a handmade surface. The lines are unerringly clean with luminous highlights from gold leaf, as well as skilled brushwork that makes for delicate shading. Burnished and flattened by being rubbed with agate, these elements become unified on a page, harmonizing together as they attain a final polish. These refined techniques were first born and developed in the Indian and Persian court ateliers of the past and have been mastered by Olivia in the present-day workshops of Jaipur, where they are still being partly practised today.

But all artistic technique is ultimately in service of an idea, and the marriage of traditional methods with a new vision is at the core of Olivia's work. Her imagery arises from an engagement with Indian yogic and meditative tradition, freshly interpreted. Lotus flowers, radial cosmic diagrams and essentialized blocks of colour speak to both the abstract and concrete symbolic language of esoteric Hinduism. Certain pure and simplified motifs are found in eighteenth- and nineteenth- century Rajput painting, when earlier generations of artists were also engaged with devotional texts and practices. While referring to the powerful painting styles of the past, Olivia's creations interpret established idioms in the light of modern aesthetic movements, including minimalism and, more remotely, surrealism, and even contemporary conceptual art.

The lotus flower has ancient roots in the art of India, its deepest association being with notions of the sacred. As a motif in art it was further renewed when it found its way back into the subcontinent through a long journey from China, via the Mongols and the Mughals, appearing as part of the language of sixteenth- and seventeenth-century arabesque ornament.

Olivia's lotus flowers and buds are most closely evocative of the eighteenth and nineteenth centuries, when Rajput paintings and pichwai temple hangings often featured a lotus-filled lake at the lowest horizontal register of a composition. The 'Breath' series recalls the lotus flower in its various incarnations, both symbolically and stylistically.

Works such as 'Darshan' or 'Rasa Lila' offer fresh interpretations of bhakti (devotional) themes, paring down iconography but staying true to the subject. Colour is a significant key to the meaning of the works, indicating deity, gender or sacred site. The titles of the works are also important in understanding them, but even if imagined separated from their nomenclature, the spirit and meaning of the paintings are quite evident. An unexpected visual meeting point with Islamic art also emerges in Olivia's spiralling radial compositions. Titled 'Churning', possibly referring to the well known subject of the churning of the cosmic ocean in Indian court painting, these movement-filled works offer a new visual interpretation of that traditional subject. However, they also evoke the formal medallions of illuminated manuscripts or spiral fluting and inner domes of Islamic buildings which share similar designs. The works of several modern and contemporary artists of the Middle East offer an interesting point of comparison.

Olivia Fraser first learned how to paint in England in a very different idiom and style. She can control oil colour on canvas, painting at a large scale with long, loose strokes. She can also paint with layers of watercolour, as various ancestors in her family did. Working on wasli (Indian paper) with pigment is yet another step in this artist's journey. Her technique may change again in the future, but her search for meaning is a constant.

NAVINA HAIDAR

Diwali, 2007
(OF0796)

Bakri, 2008
(OF0803)

Cockerels, 2009
(OF0902)

Dawn, 2012
(OF1202)

Desert, 2012
(OF1204)

Golden Lotus, 2008
(OF0802)

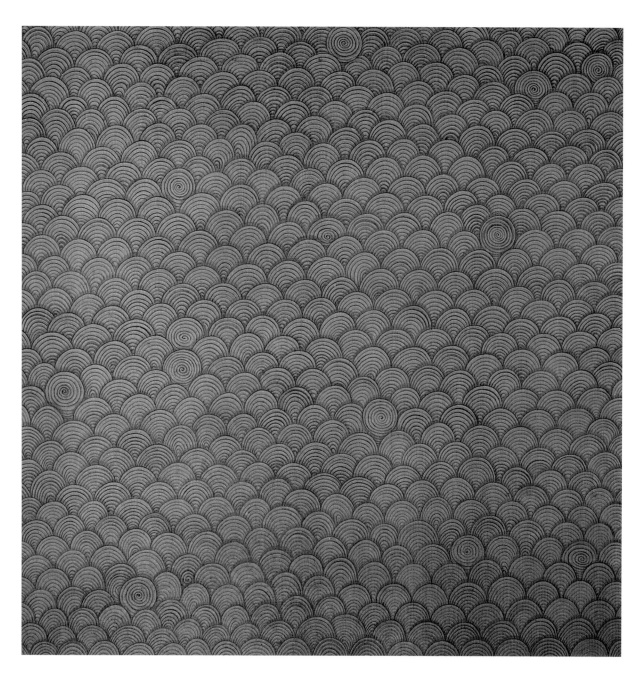
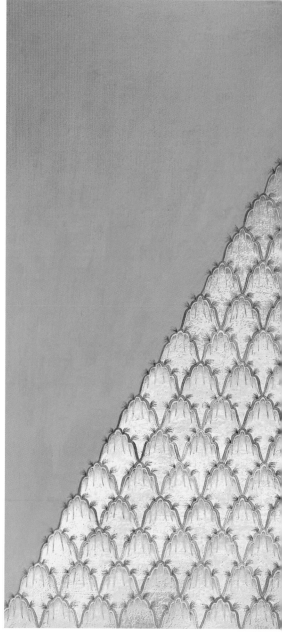

Mount Meru (Triptych), 2010
(OF1003)

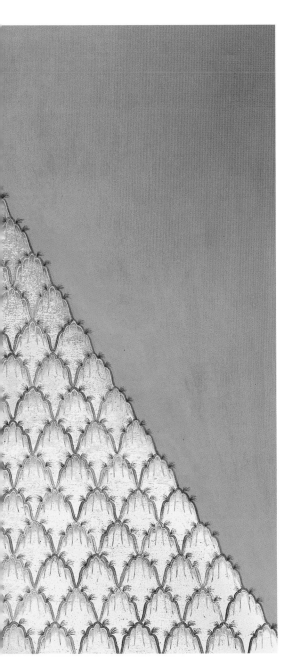

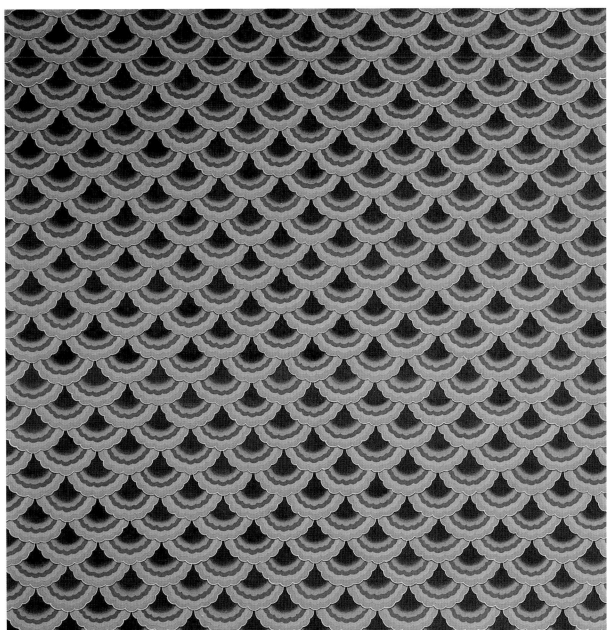

Pilgrimage, 2011
(OF1101)

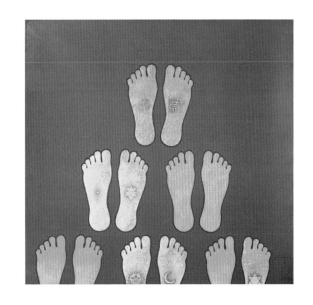

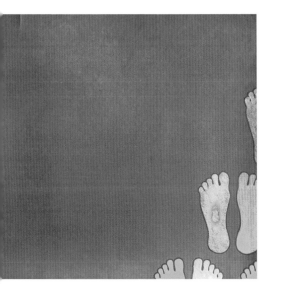
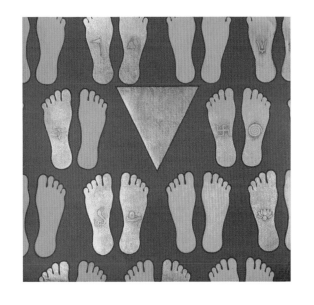
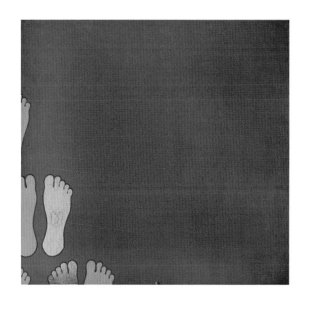
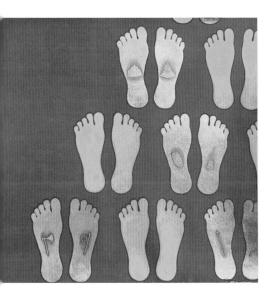
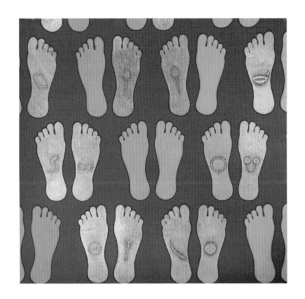
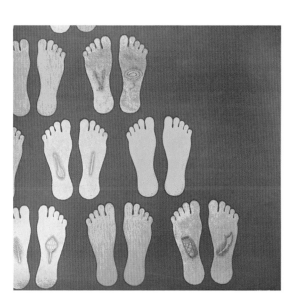

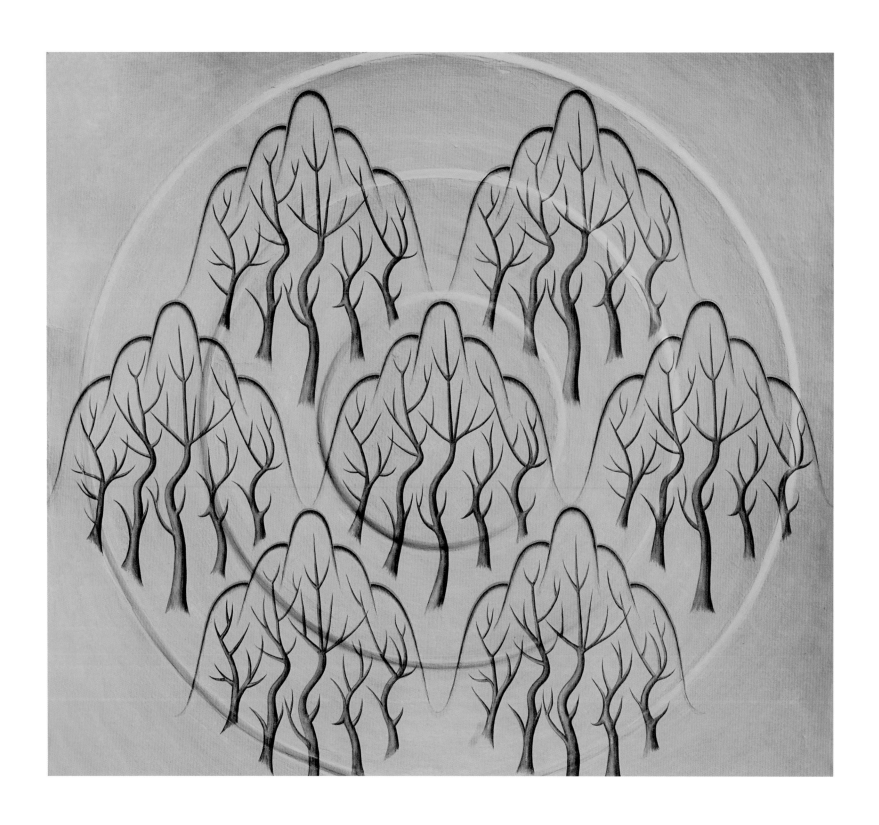

Holy Mountain, 2011
(OF1110)

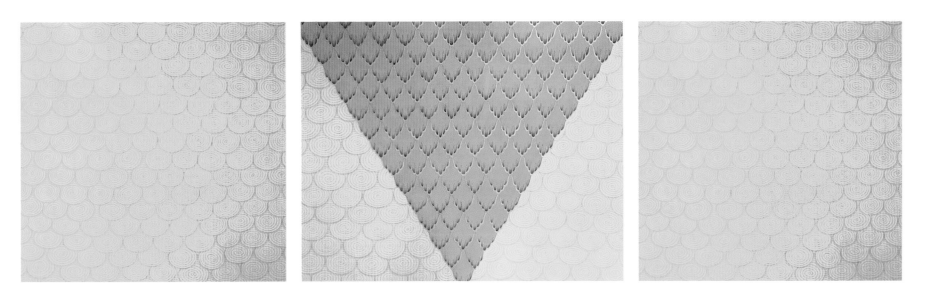

Churning of the Milky Ocean, 2011
(OF1111)

67

Creation, 2011
(OF1103)

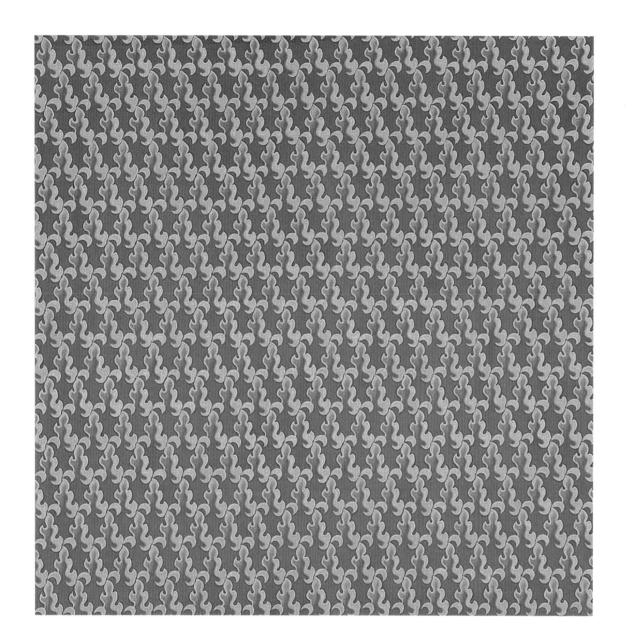
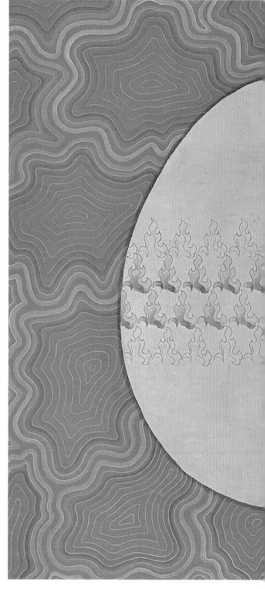

Genesis (Triptych), 2011
(OF1109)

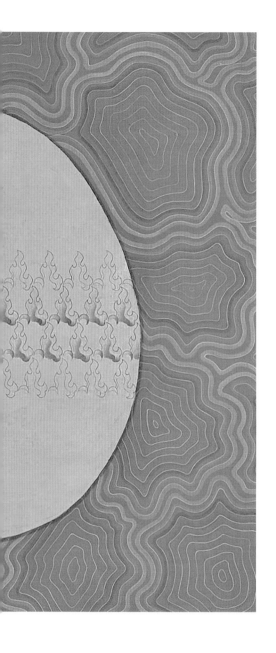

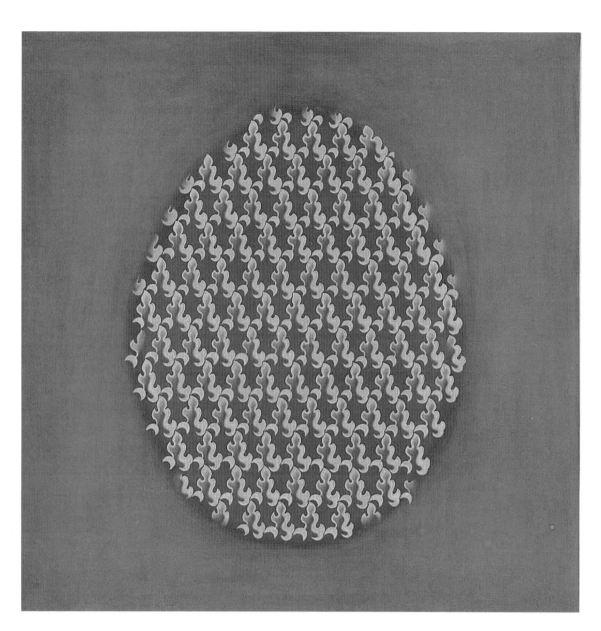

Essence, 2012
(OF1205)

The Elements, 2012
(OF1206)

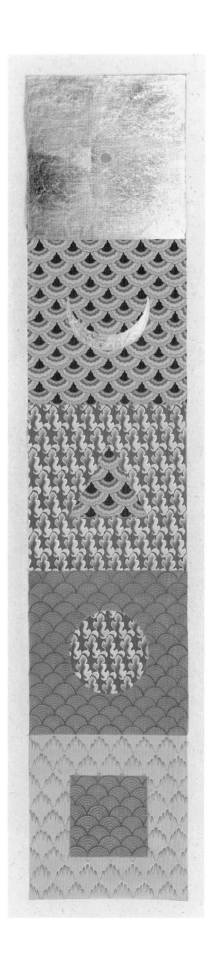

Dissolution, 2012
(OF1207)

You Drew Forth the Sun That Was Hidden in the Water - Rigveda 10.7, 2011
(OF1102)

River Raag, 2013
(OF1310)

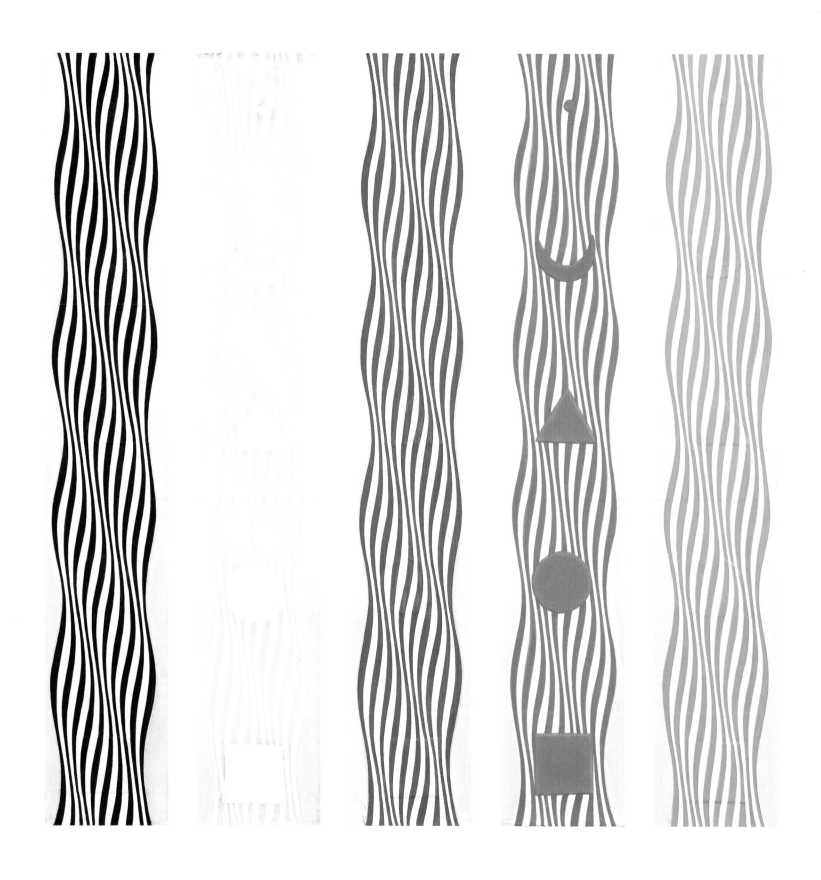

River of Life, 2012
(OF1210)

River of Life, 2014
(OF1403)

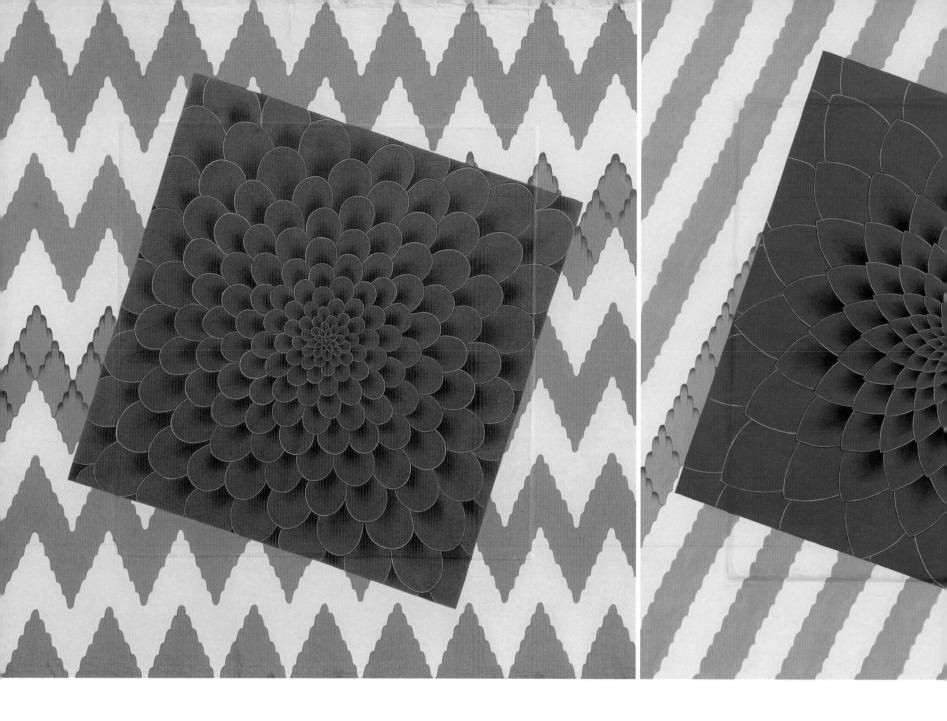

Himalaya, 2013
(OF1304)

Blue Himalaya, 2015
(OF1505)

Red Himalaya, 2015
(OF1516)

Churning I, 2015
(OF1506)

Churning II, 2015
(OF1507)

Jambudvipa, 2017
(OF1707)

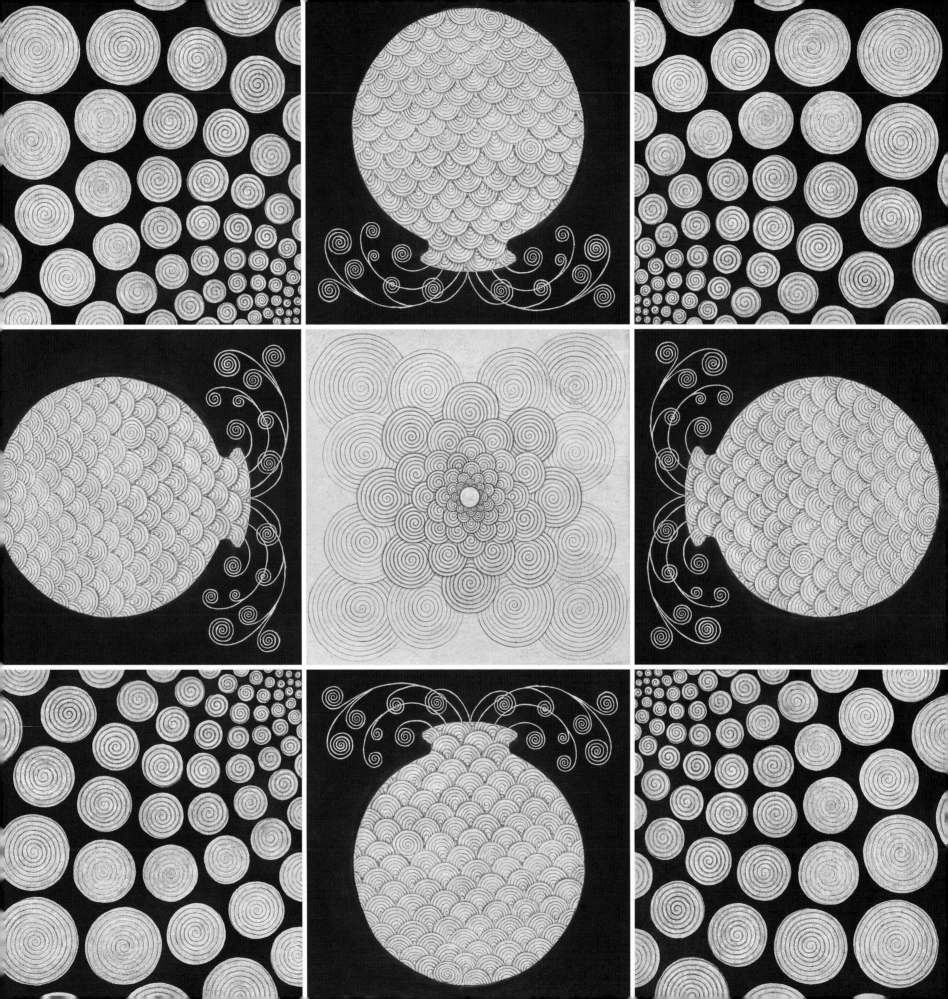

THE
LOTUS WITHIN

The Lotus Within

Late in the Gheranda Samhita, an early eighteenth-century Sanskrit yoga treatise, advice is given concerning visualization; the practice of envisaging landscapes in order to enhance the profundity of meditation achieved by the yogi:

The yogi should visualize a sublime ocean of nectar in his heart, with an island of jewels in its middle whose sand is made of gemstones. In every direction there are kadamba trees with abundant flowers ... where the scents of malati, mallika, jati and sthalapadma flowers perfume every quarter ... Bees and cuckoos buzz and call there.

The yogi should visualize a lotus attached to the pericarp of the great thousand-petalled lotus. It is white, luminous and has twelve seed syllables: ha, sa, ksha, ma, la, va, ra, yum, ha, sa, kha, and phrem, in that order.

These extraordinary passages are clearly painterly in their way of seeing. Their pristinated language, and what we might now call the hyper-realism of the attention they practise (the impossible noticing of every scent, every sound, every syllable), summons glinting dreamscapes into being. More precisely, their imagery and technique also closely echo the Indian miniature tradition of art from the seventeenth and eighteenth centuries, with its lapidary investment in both the luminous and the numinous as they manifest in the living world.

Olivia Fraser's remarkable recent work grows out of her deep engagement with both golden-age Indian miniaturism and ancient forms of hatha yoga to which visualization is central. Her skills in both of these traditions are formidable. She has spent years as an apprentice to the miniaturist masters, learning the 'many layers and regulations' that guide the making of this art and years exploring the literature and techniques of yoga. The resulting art does not only imagine landscapes, it contains landscapes. Elements of place itself have been crushed, mixed and polished into these paintings: white chalk from the cliffs in Jaipur, nuts and sap gathered from trees, malachite ground to a glowing green powder. As the animals of Lascaux were present in the paint before they were painted on the chamber walls (there as 'bone-black' and binding fat), the more-than-human world is present in Fraser's art before it is even laid down.

These are 'visionary' works in the non-trivial sense of the word. They are born in the mind's eye of the artist and they re-focus the mind's eye of the viewer. On first seeing 'The Scent of the Lotus II', in which a swarm of golden bees radiate in towards a central golden lotus blossom, I found myself drawn – no, pulled – into the image by its great centripetal force, and I also seemed to hear or feel, at some deep internal level, the vibration of the bees' wings as they move with order and urgency to their goal. 'On hearing the sound of a bee from within', declares the Gheranda Samhita, 'lead the mind there.'

Pinwheels and starbursts, constellations and soul maps, slow unfurlings and rich pulsations – Fraser's work somehow possesses at once a calm grace and a hallucinatory intensity. She practises what Glenn Lowry, director of the Museum of Modern Art in New York, has called 'elaboration by simplification ... they are no longer details magnified but details transformed'. The result is a hugely powerful body of work that – to quote again from the Gheranda Samhita – 'puts the self in space and space in the self.'

ROBERT MACFARLANE
June 2018

Awakening, 2012
(OF1201)

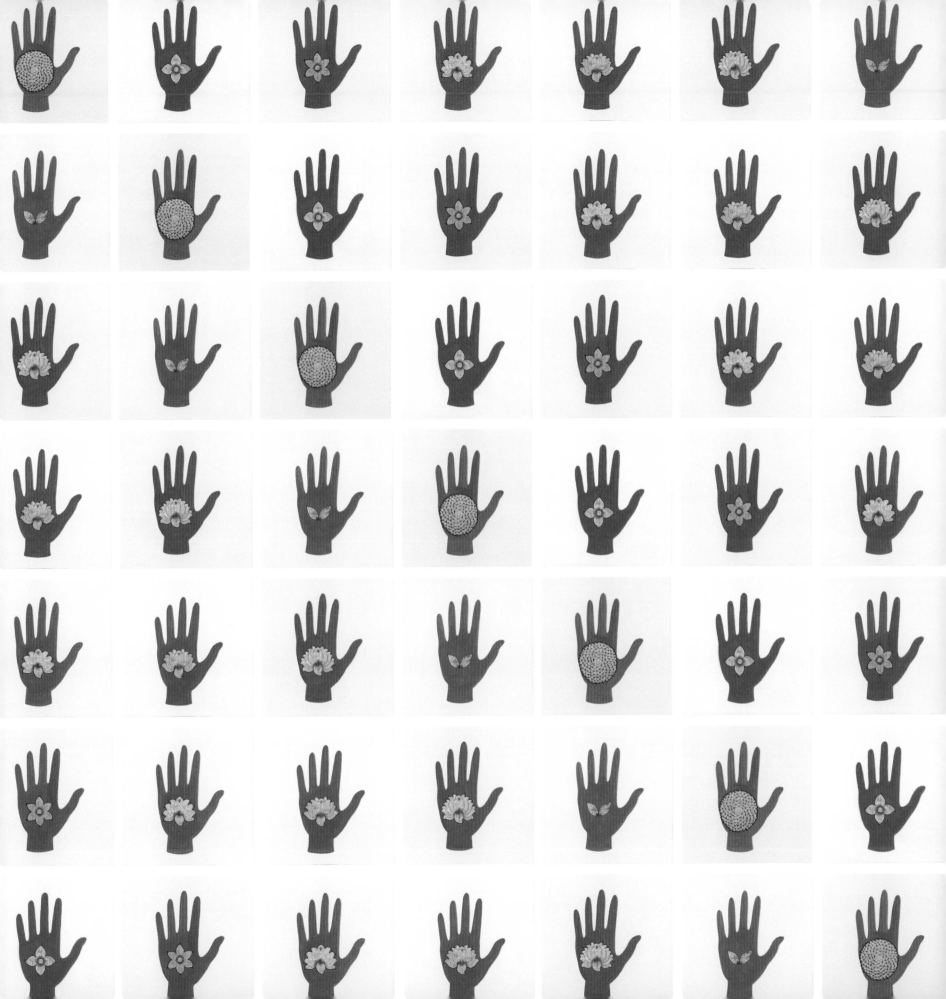

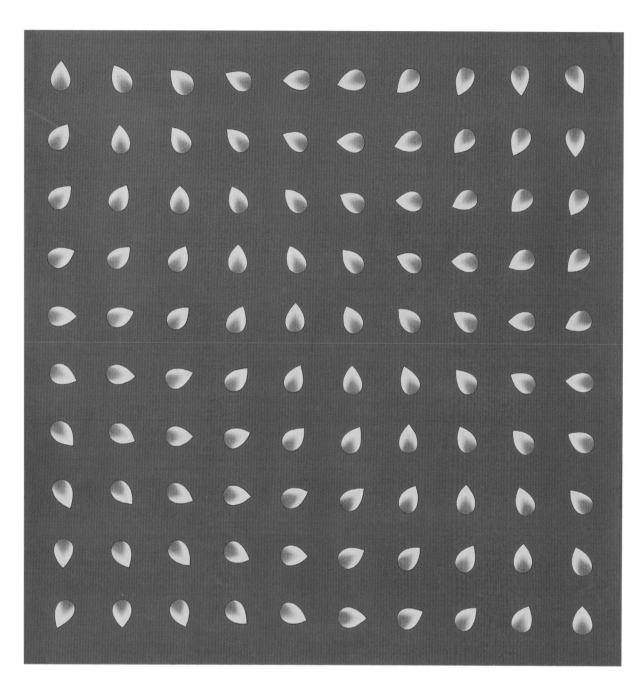

Chakra I, 2013
(OF1307)

Chakra III, 2013
(OF1309)

Chakra II, 2013
(OF1308)

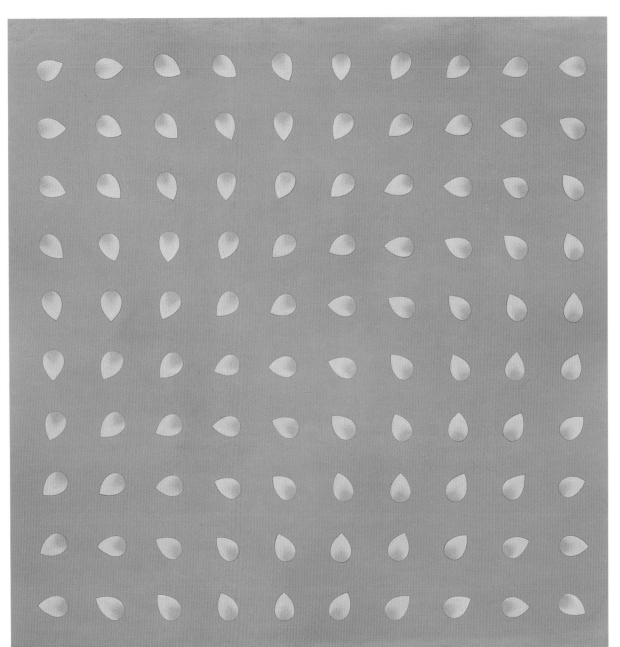

Kundalini I, 2014
(OF1401)

Kundalini II, 2014
(OF1449)

Darshan, 2012
(OF1209)

Lotus Eyed, 2013
(OF1303)

Yantra, 2014
(OF1404)

1000 Petals, 2013
(OF1305)

The Seven Chakras, 2019
(OF1905)

Darshan II, 2015
(OF1501)

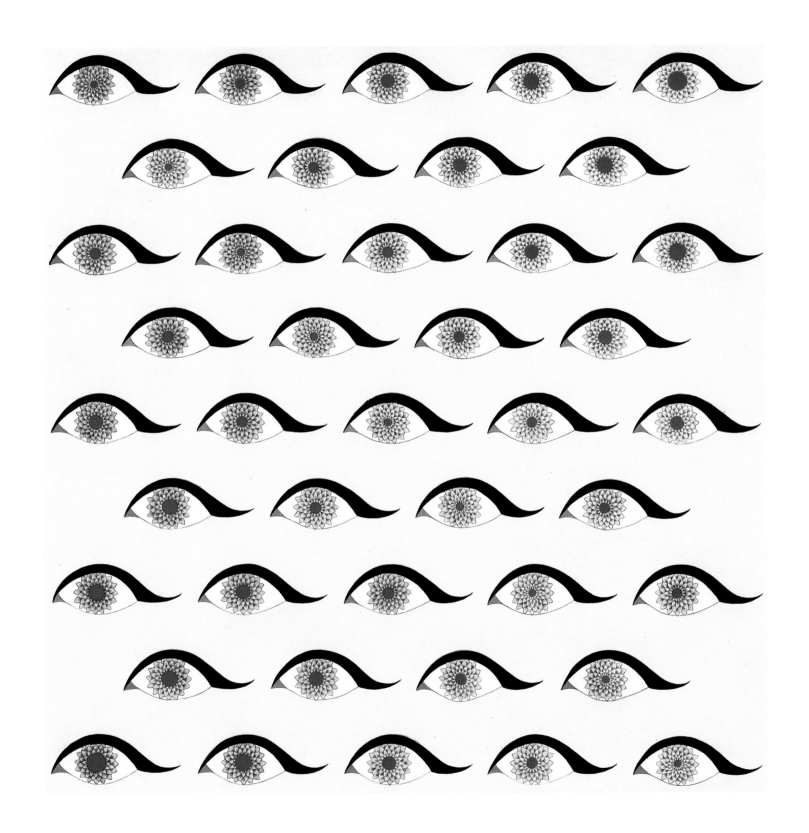

Darshan, 2015
(OF1504)

Breath, 2015
(OF1510)

Breathe, 2015
(OF1511)

Prana, 2015
(OF1513)

Breathe, 2016
(OF1605)

110

Breathe II, 2017
(OF1702)

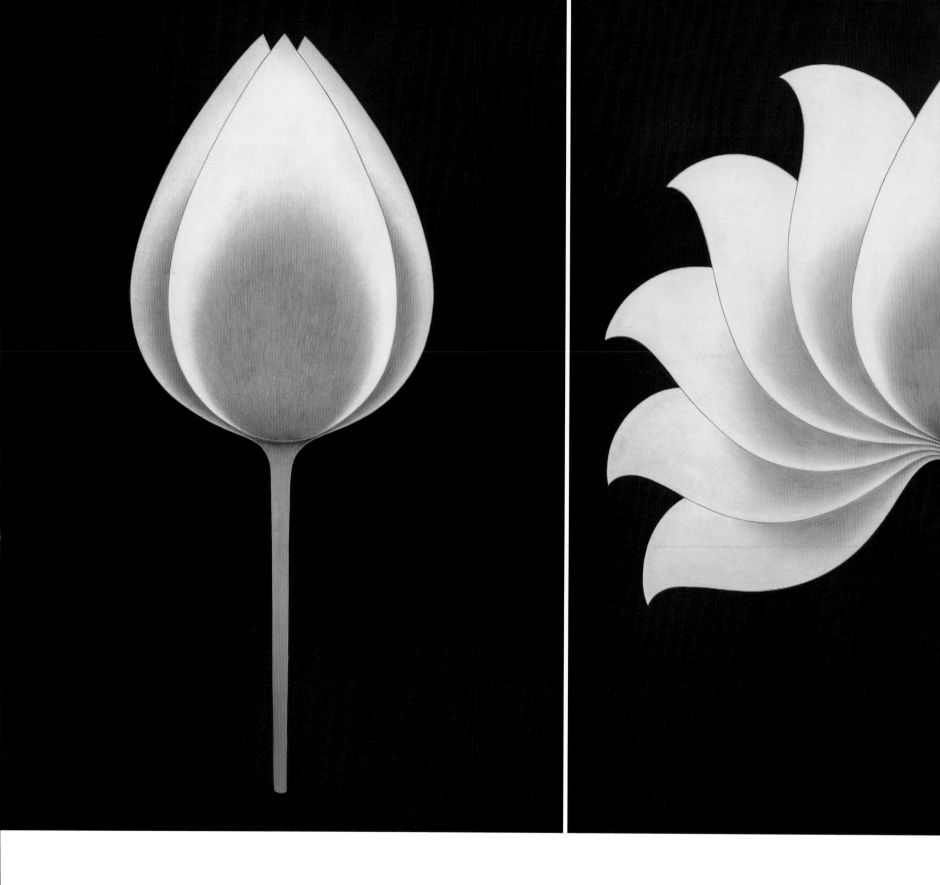

Breath, 2016
(OF1606)

Breath II, 2016
(OF1601)

Breath III, 2019
(OF1904)

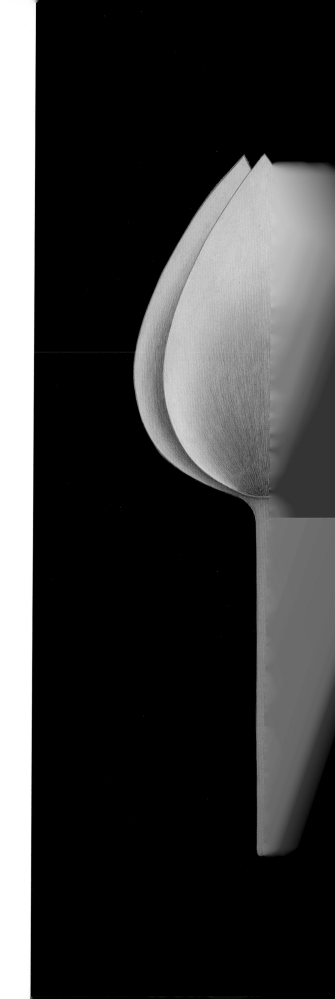

Pause II, 2016
(OF1604)

Chakras, 2015
(OF1520)

Chakras, 2017
(OF1703)

Porous Borders, 2015
(OF1521)

The Golden Lotus, 2017
(OF1704)

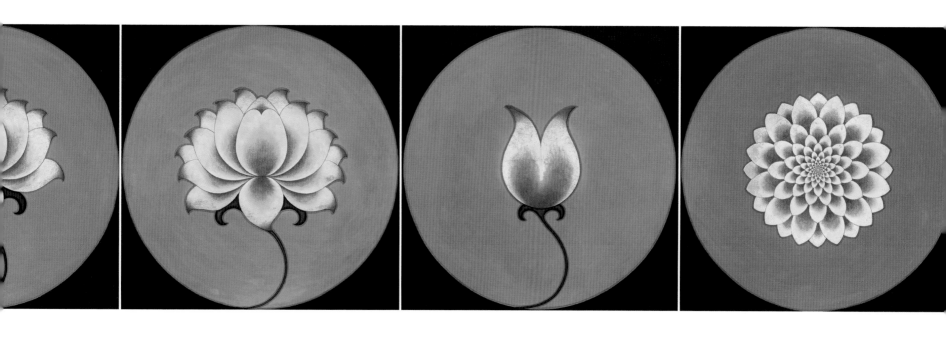

Sthalapadma, 2017
(OF1706)

Neelkamal, 2019
(OF1906)

(following spread)

Darshan II, 2018
(OF1802)

THE
COSMOS

Kalachakra, 2016
(OF1607)

I am the Moon, 2015
(OF1509)

134

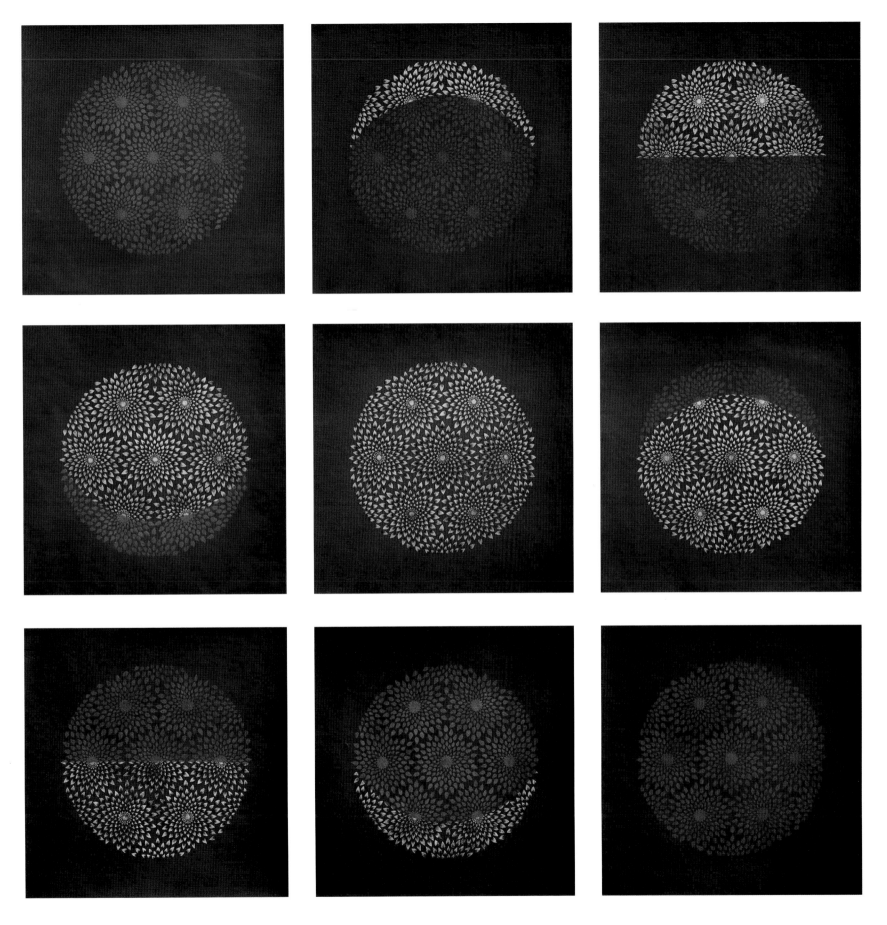

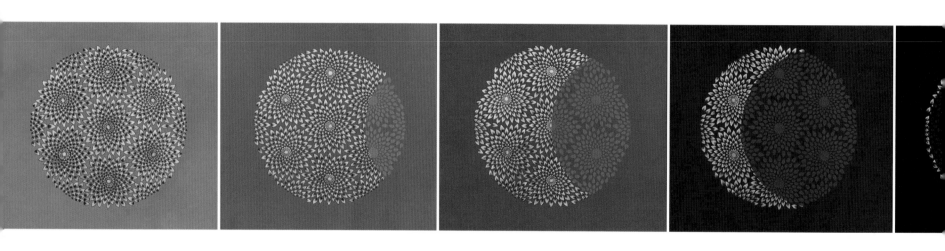

You are the Sun, 2015
(OF1512)

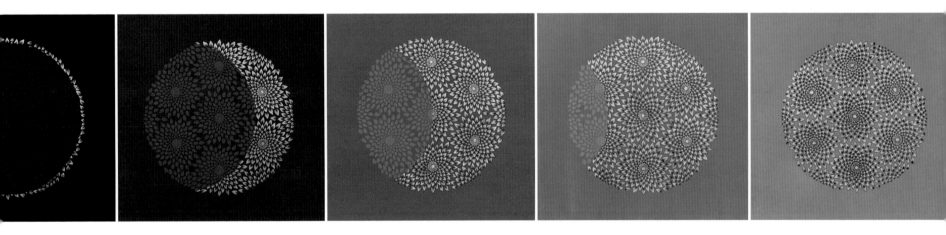

(following spread)

Sun, 2013
(OF1301)

Moon, 2013
(OF1302)

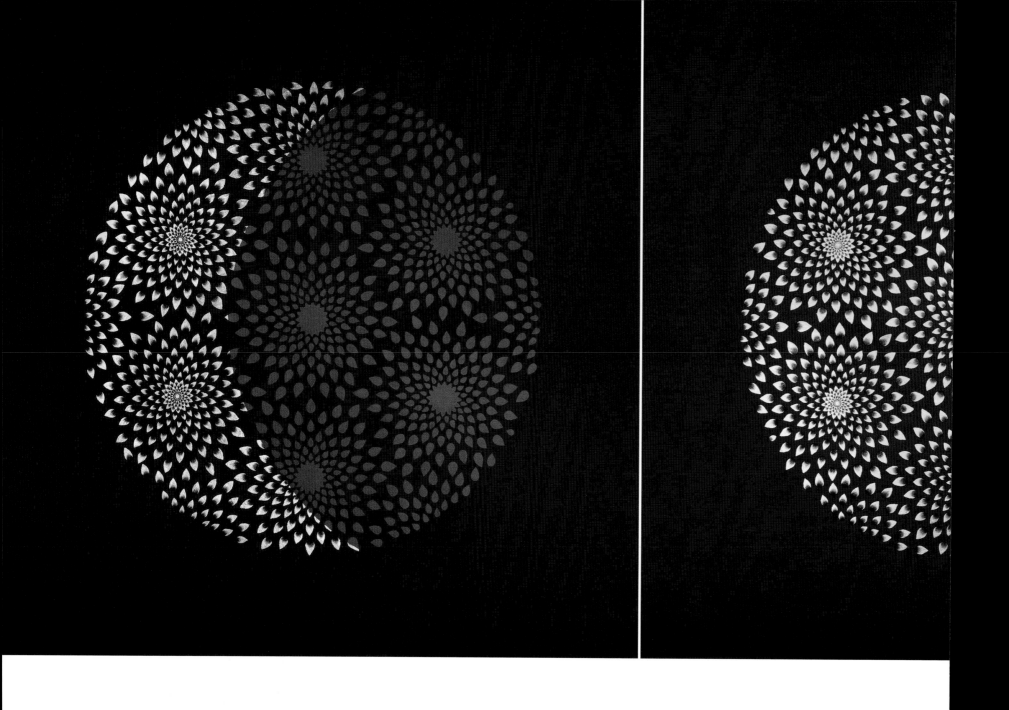

Moon (Triptych), 2017-2018
(OF1807)

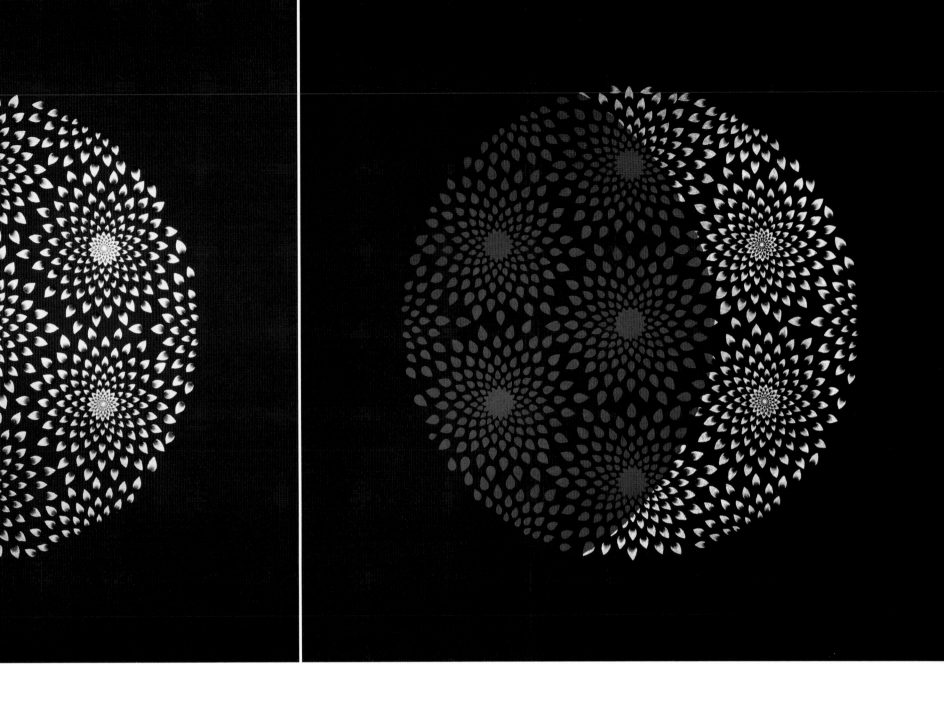

(preceding spread)

White Star, 2017
(OF1701)

Black Star, 2017
(OF1705)

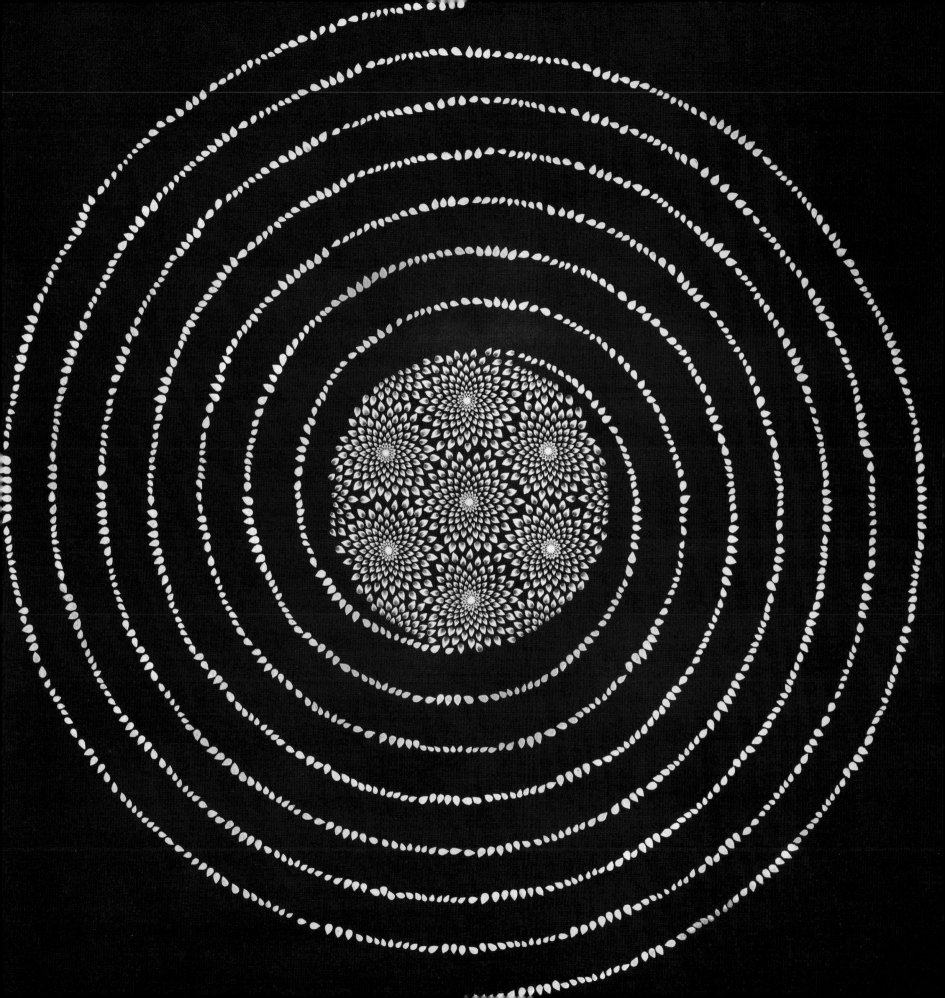

(preceding spread)

Constellation, 2018
(OF1808)

Creation, 2018
(OF1806)

New Moon, 2018
(OF1803)

AMRIT

(opposite page)

Scent of the Lotus III, 2018
(OF1810)

(preceding spread)

(following spread)

Scent of the Lotus I, 2018
(OF1805)

Scent of the Lotus IV, 2018
(OF1811)

Scent of The Lotus II, 2018
(OF1804)

Scent of the Lotus V, 2018
(OF1812)

154

Amrit, 2018
(OF1813)

Metamorphosis I, 2018
(OF1814)

Metamorphosis II, 2018
(OF1815)

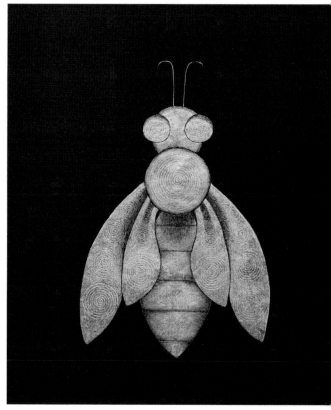

Bhramari (Triptych), 2019
(OF1901)

Kama (Diptych), 2019
(OF1902)

A Partnership

It was back in 2011 that Virginia Whiles suggested I look at the work of a British artist working in Delhi. At the time, the Grosvenor Gallery was already working with several contemporary Indian artists whose market had just crashed, so we weren't really looking to add another to the gallery's portfolio. Nevertheless, I decided to make the torturous journey to Olivia's home and studio at Mira Singh's farm on the outskirts of New Delhi. On seeing the works, any concerns I had vanished, and over a good cup of chai, I promptly offered Olivia a group show in London. I discovered Peter Nagy had likewise offered Olivia a group show at his gallery Nature Morte in New Delhi, and from these new collaborative beginnings over the last eight years, Olivia's artistic career has gone from strength to strength.

The Grosvenor Gallery presented its first solo exhibition of Olivia's works in 2012 and has shown her works at numerous international art fairs, and just last year followed with another triumphant solo show, 'The Lotus Within'. Other highlights include her exhibition in New York (2016), the Venice Biennale (2015), Shanghai (2014) and Goa (2013). A special mention needs to be given to Olivia's first museum show in India at the Government Museum & Art Gallery in Chandigarh in 2016. This was possible through the wonderful support and encouragement of Professor B.N Goswamy, one of the greatest experts on Pahari and Indian miniature painting.

The level of interest in Olivia's work over the last few years has grown to such a point that a book documenting her oeuvre was needed, and here we are.

The production of this book was possible through the help of the many involved. Firstly, my thanks go to all the academics, journalists and art professionals whose essays on Olivia's work are included in this book, namely Virginia Whiles, Navina Haidar, Robert Macfarlane and B.N. Goswamy. Secondly, I wish to thank Peter Nagy and Aparajita Jain of Nature Morte for organising Olivia's current exhibition, as well as to Olivia's New York dealer Sundaram Tagore of Sundaram Tagore Gallery. Thirdly, the publishers HarperCollins India, namely Ananth Padmanabhan and Bonita Shimray for their collaboration on this venture. Fourthly, to the team at Grosvenor Gallery, especially Kajoli Khanna, for documenting the works and pulling all the information together for this book. Lastly, and by no means least, thanks to all the collectors whose continued support and love for Olivia's work have created the need for a book of this nature.

Finally, congratulations Olivia on your exhibition and this wonderful book. You have been an absolute pleasure to work with over these past years and you deserve every success.

CONOR MACKLIN
Grosvenor Gallery

OLIVIA FRASER

Olivia Fraser (b. 1965)

After graduating with an MA in Modern Languages from Oxford, Olivia spent a year at Wimbledon Art College before moving to India in 1989.

Following in the footsteps of her kinsman, James Baillie Fraser, who painted India's monuments and landscape in the early 1800s, Olivia set out to continue where he left off, painting the architecture of Delhi and its people. James Baillie Fraser also commissioned local artists to paint what has become the famous 'Fraser Album', which influenced Olivia's early work during the 1990s.

In 2005, she decided to study the traditional Indian miniature painting techniques under Jaipuri and Delhi masters and now applies them to her work using gem-like stone colours, unique miniature brush work and elaborate decorative and burnished surfaces. Having been especially influenced by Nathdwara pichwai painting and early nineteenth-century Jodhpuri painting, Olivia has been exploring their visual language, reaching back to an archetypal iconography strongly rooted in India's artistic and cultural heritage that has helped her integrate influences from both the East as well as the West.

Her latest body of work is deeply rooted in her fascination with and practice of yoga and the ways in which yogic meditation involves visualizations of the garden, particularly the sahasrara, or thousand-petaled lotus, which serves as a visual aid in reaching enlightenment.

Olivia's paintings have been shown in various galleries and art fairs around the world. They are also included in collections in India (Kiran Nadar Museum of Art), the UK, France, Belgium (Museum of Sacred Art), UAE, Singapore, Australia, China (China Arts Museum) and the USA. Olivia's works were shown as part of Frontiers Reimagined, a collateral event of the 56th Venice Biennale in 2015.

Olivia divides her time between Delhi and London.

SOLO SHOWS

2019 Olivia Fraser: Amrit, 25 October – 22 November 2019, Nature Morte, New Delhi

2018 Olivia Fraser: The Lotus Within, 6 – 26 June 2018, Grosvenor Gallery, London

2017 Anahat, Solo booth at Art Dubai, Dubai, UAE

2016 Olivia Fraser: Sacred Garden, The Government Museum & Art Gallery, Chandigarh, India

2016 The Sacred Garden, Sundaram Tagore, New York

2014 India Art Fair, Grosvenor Gallery Solo Booth, New Delhi, India

2014 Subtle Bodies, in association with Art 18/21, Norwich

2014 Olivia Fraser, M on the Bund, Shanghai, China

2013 Sunaparanta Centre for the Arts, Goa, India

2012 Miniatures, Grosvenor Gallery, London, UK

2007 Triveni Gallery, New Delhi, India

2003 Indar Pasricha Fine Art, London, UK

1998 Indar Pasricha Fine Art, London, UK

1994 Andrew Usiskin Fine Art, London, UK

1991 Carma Galleries, New Delhi, India

GROUP SHOWS

2019 The Monsoon Festival 13, curated by Red Earth at City Palace, Jaipur

2019 Cabinet of Curiosities: Red Earth Design Mela at KK Square, Jaipur

2019 Cabinet of Curiosities: Red Earth Design Mela at Coomaraswamy Hall, Mumbai, 13 – 14 April 2019

2019 India Art Fair, Grosvenor Gallery Booth, New Delhi

2018 The Art of Paper, 15 November – 15 December 2018, Sundaram Tagore, New York

2018 Prakash Parv: The Festival of Light, 2 – 4 November 2018, Alliance Francaise, New Delhi

2018 Luminously Between Eternities, 1 – 21 December, Gallery Ark, Gujarat

2018 The Monsoon Festival 13, 2 – 16 September, City Palace, Jaipur

2018 Paradox and Play: Living Traditions in Contemporary Art, New Delhi

2018 India Art Fair, Grosvenor Gallery Booth, New Delhi

2017 India Art Fair, Grosvenor Gallery Booth, New Delhi

2016 India Art Fair, Grosvenor Gallery Booth, New Delhi

2016 Deck of Cards, British Council, New Delhi

2015 Unfolding Perspectives, Deck gallery, Singapore

2016 Gandhara Art, Art Basel Hong Kong

2015 Frontiers Reimagined, Venice Biennale

2015 Yoga Chakra, LKA, New Delhi

2015 Forms of Devotion, China Arts Museum, Shanghai

2015 Grosvenor Gallery, India Art Fair, New Delhi

2014 Kullu Perceived, The Prince's Drawing School, London

2013 Modern & Contemporary Miniatures: Grosvenor Gallery, London

2013 Miniature Rewind: Art Dubai

2013 Grosvenor Gallery, India Art Fair, New Delhi

2012 Asian Art in London

2012 Iconographic Investigations: Nature Morte, Gurgaon

2012 Interrogating Conventions: Nature Morte, New Delhi

2012 Grosvenor Gallery, India Art Fair, New Delhi

2011 The Path of the Lotus: Grosvenor Gallery, London

2010 Kathmandu Arts Centre, Nepal

2010 Apparao Galleries, Chennai

2009 Apparao Galleries, New Delhi

2008 Kathmandu Arts Centre, Nepal

2004 Presteigne Art Gallery, Wales

1999 The Portland Gallery, London

1996 The Clarendon Gallery, London

Afsal Khan's Tomb, 1990
Watercolour on paper
(OF9002)

The Times of India, 1991
Watercolour on paper
(OF9101)

Juggi, 1991
Watercolour on paper
(OF9105)

Chai Stall, 1990
Watercolour on paper
(OF9003)

Humayun's Tomb, 1991
Watercolour on paper
(OF9103)

Card Players, 1991
Watercolour on paper
(OF9106)

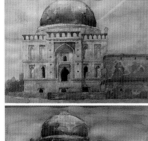

Lodhi Gardens I & II, 1990
Watercolour on paper
(OF9006) | (OF9007)

Untitled, 1991
Watercolour on paper
(OF9104)

Dancing Girl, 1991
Watercolour on paper
(OF9107)

Safdarjung's Tomb, 'City of Djinns', 1991
Watercolour on paper
(OF9108)

Sufis at the Shrine, 1991
Watercolour on paper
(OF9111)

Jharoka, 1993
Watercolour on paper
(OF9303)

Jodhpur Fort Rajasthan, 1991
Watercolour on paper
(OF9109)

Untitled, 1991
Watercolour on paper
(OF9112)

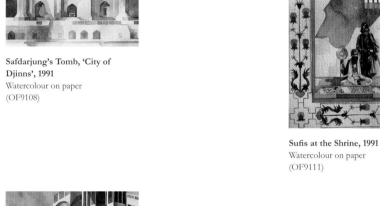

Jama Masjid, 1993
Watercolour on paper
(OF9304)

Chattri, Purana Qila, Delhi, 1991
Watercolour on paper
(OF9110)

Untitled, 1991
Watercolour on paper
(OF9113)

Golconda, 1998
Watercolour on paper
76.5 x 38 cm | 30 1/8 x 15 in
(OF9803)

Untitled , 1991
Watercolour on paper
(OF9114)

Two Jaisalmeri Men, 1992
Watercolour on paper
(OF9201)

Sadhu, 1992
Watercolour on paper
(OF9206)

Untitled , 1991
Watercolour on paper
(OF9115)

Two Women, 1992
Watercolour on paper
(OF9203)

Roadside Barber, 1992
Watercolour on paper
(OF9207)

Untitled , 1991
Watercolour on paper
(OF9116)

Kwality Ice Cream, 1992
Watercolour on paper
(OF9205)

Taxi Stand, 1992
Watercolour on paper
(OF9208)

Women at Work, 1992
Watercolour on paper
(OF9210)

Fishermen, Goa, 1992
Watercolour on paper
(OF9214)

Rooftop Nursery, 1992
Watercolour on paper
(OF9217)

Two Sikhs with Pigeons, 1992
Watercolour on paper
(OF9211)

Three Men, 1992
Watercolour on paper
(OF9215)

Rickshaw Wallah, 1992
Watercolour on paper
(OF9218)

Three Men, 1992
Watercolour on paper
(OF9213)

Partridge Fight, 1992
Watercolour on paper
(OF9216)

Man with a Hookah, 1992
Watercolour on paper
(OF9219)

Paan Shop, 1992
Watercolour on paper
(OF9220)

Untitled, 1992
Watercolour on paper
(OF9223)

Untitled , 1992
Watercolour on paper
(OF9226)

Untitled, 1992
Watercolour on paper
(OF9221)

Rajasthani Women and Baby, 1992
Watercolour on paper
(OF9224)

Rajasthani Couple, 1992
Watercolour on paper
(OF9227)

Untitled , 1992
Watercolour on paper
(OF9222)

Untitled , 1992
Watercolour on paper
(OF9225)

The Temple Tap, 1992
Watercolour on paper
(OF9228)

Untitled , 1992
Watercolour on paper
(OF9229)

Card Players, 1993
Watercolour on paper
(OF9305)

Untitled, 1993
Watercolour on paper
(OF9309)

Holymans Pupils, 1992
Watercolour on paper
(OF9301)

Gossip, 1993
Watercolour on paper
(OF9306)

Humayuns Tomb, 1993
Watercolour on paper
(OF9311)

The Pearl Mosque, Age of Kali, 1993
Watercolour on paper
(OF9302)

Chapatti Maker, 1993
Watercolour on paper
(OF9307)

Lodhi Tomb, 1993
Watercolour on paper
(OF9312)

Group of Women, 1994
Watercolour on paper
(OF9401)

Blue Mosque Istanbul, 1996
Watercolour on paper
(OF9601)

Gypsy Girls in Goa , 1998
Watercolour on paper
(OF9804)

Purana Qila, 1995
Watercolour on paper
(OF9501)

The Musicians, 1998
Watercolour on paper
21.7 x 21.7 cm | 8 1/2 x 8 1/2 in
(OF9801)

Zebra Crossing, 1998
Watercolour on paper
17.2 x 20 cm | 6 3/4 x 7 7/8 in
(OF9805)

Safdarjung's Tomb, 1995
Watercolour on paper
(OF9502)

Taxi Stand, 1998
Watercolour on paper
18.5 x 18.5 cm | 7 1/4 x 7 1/4 in
(OF9802)

The Dehradun Express, 1998
Watercolour on paper
17.1 x 17.1 cm | 6 3/4 x 6 3/4 in
(OF9806)

Rajdhani Express, 1998
Watercolour on paper
18.4 x 18.1 cm | 7 1/4 x 7 1/8 in
(OF9807)

The Barber Shop, 1998
Watercolour on paper
23.3 x 19.4 cm | 9 1/8 x 7 5/8 in
(OF9811)

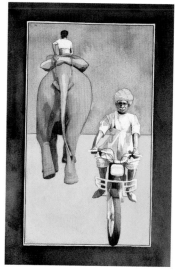

The Motorbike, 1999
Watercolour on paper
(OF9903)

New Dehli Railway Station, 1998
Watercolour on paper
18 x 18 cm | 7 1/8 x 7 1/8 in
(OF9809)

Durga Ice Cream, 1999
Watercolour on paper
(OF9901)

Sugar Cane Wallah, 1999
Watercolour on paper
13 x 11.5 cm | 5 1/8 x 4 1/2 in
(OF9904)

Lodhi Gardens New Delhi , 1998
Watercolour on paper
18.2 x 18.6 cm | 7 1/8 x 7 3/8 in
(OF9810)

Dood Wallahs, 1999
Watercolour on paper
(OF9902)

Sisters in law, 1999
Watercolour on paper
11.5 x 10 cm | 4 1/2 x 4 in
(OF9905)

Vegetable Sellers, 1999
Watercolour on paper
27.6 x 20 cm | 10 7/8 x 7 7/8 in
(OF9906)

Dhobi Wllah, 1999
Watercolour on paper
(OF9909)

Jama Masjid, 1999
Watercolour on paper
(OF9912)

Tempo, 1999
Watercolour on paper
(OF9913)

Jodhpuri Dancers, 1999
Watercolour on paper
(OF9907)

Tailor, 1999
Watercolour on paper
(OF9910)

Kabootar Baz, 1999
Watercolour on paper
(OF9914)

Man Smoking Hookah, 1999
Watercolour on paper
(OF9908)

Sadehu, 1999
Watercolour on paper
(OF9911)

The Partridge Fight, 1999
Watercolour on paper
(OF9915)

Chapattis, 2000
Watercolour on paper
17.1 x 17.1 cm | 6 3/4 x 6 3/4 in
(OF0001)

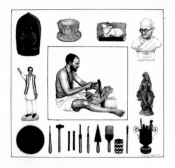

Brahmin Sculptor, 2000
Watercolour on paper
19.1 x 19.1 cm | 7 1/2 x 7 1/2 in
(OF0005)

The Milkman, 2001
Watercolour on paper
(OF0104)

Wool Gatherers, 2000
Watercolour on paper
29.2 x 26.7 cm | 11 1/2 x 10 1/2 in
(OF0002)

Railway Clock, 2001
Watercolour on paper
(OF0101)

Rama, Hanuman, Sita, 2001
Watercolour on paper
(OF0105)

Dhobi Wallahs, 2000
Watercolour on paper
(OF0003)

Rice Pickers, 2001
Watercolour on paper
(OF0102)

Goat Herds, 2001
Watercolour on paper
(OF0106)

Street I, 2001
Watercolour on paper
(OF0107)

Singing the 'Phad', 2001
Watercolour on paper
(OF0110)

The Boy with the Flute, 2001
Watercolour on paper
(OF0113)

Street II, 2001
Watercolour on paper
(OF0108)

Yatra, 2001
Watercolour on paper
(OF0111)

Banjara Women II, 2002
Watercolour on paper
(OF0201)

Street III, 2001
Watercolour on paper
(OF0109)

Bollywood Babe - Soha Ali Khan, 2001
Watercolour on paper
(OF0112)

Lodhi Gardens Morning, 2002
Watercolour on paper
(OF0215)

Paban das Baul I, 2003
Watercolour on paper
(OF0301)

Wedding Procession, 2003
Watercolour on paper
(OF0304)

Brick Makers, 2003
Watercolour on paper
(OF0307)

Paban das Baul II, 2003
Watercolour on paper
(OF0302)

Fisherfolk, 2003
Watercolour on paper
19.1 x 19.1 cm | 7 1/2 x 7 1/2 in
(OF0305)

Ragamala I, 2003
Watercolour on paper
26.7 x 21.6 cm | 10 1/2 x 8 1/2 in
(OF0308)

Paper-Mache Idol Maker, 2003
Watercolour on paper
(OF0303)

Road Builders, 2003
Watercolour on paper
(OF0306)

The Well, 2003
Watercolour on paper
(OF0309)

The Tin Bucket Maker, 2003
Watercolour on paper
(OF0310)

Bara Gumbad, Lodhi Gardens, New Delhi, 2005
Watercolour on paper
(OF0502)

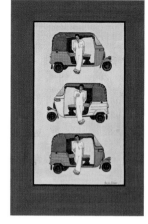

Patriotic Autos, 2006
Watercolour on paper
(OF0602)

Patachitra Painters, Orissa, 2003
Watercolour on paper
(OF0311)

The Itmad-ud-Daulah, 2005
Watercolour on paper
(OF0503)

Gopashtami (Triptych), 2007
Stone pigments, Arabic gum and gold leaf
on handmade Sanganer paper
61.3 x 31.1 cm | 24 1/8 x 12 1/4 in (each)
61.3 x 93.9 cm | 24 1/8 x 37 in (overall)
(OF0701)

Humayun's Tomb, 2005
Watercolour on paper
(OF0501)

Dance of the Peacocks (Bagicha Ka Utsava), 2006
Stone pigments, Arabic gum and gold leaf on handmade Sanganer paper
50.8 x 35.5 cm | 20 x 14 in
(OF0601)

Delhi, 2007
Watercolour on paper
22.9 x 104.1 cm | 9 x 41 in
(OF0703)

Ragamala II, 2007
Watercolour on paper
(OF0704)

Golden Lotus, 2008
Stone pigments, Arabic gum and gold
leaf on handmade Sanganer paper
48.2 x 48.2 cm | 19 x 19 in
(OF0802)

Shiva, 2009
Stone pigments and Arabic gum on
handmade Sanganer paper
73.6 x 45.7 cm | 29 x 18 in
(OF0901)

Diwali, 2007
Stone pigments and Arabic gum on
handmade Sanganer paper
21 x 30 cm | 8 1/4 x 11 3/4 in
(OF0796)

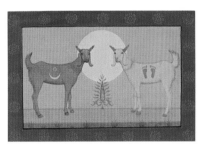

Bakri, 2008
Stone pigments and Arabic gum on
handmade Sanganer paper
21.5 x 31.7 cm | 8 1/2 x 12 1/2 in
(OF0803)

Cockerels, 2009
Stone pigments and Arabic gum on
handmade Sanganer paper
21 x 30 cm | 8 1/4 x 11 3/4 in
(OF0902)

Krishna's Garden, 2008
Stone pigments, Arabic gum and gold
leaf on handmade Sanganer paper
45.7 x 71.12 cm | 18 x 28 in
(OF0801)

Your Eyes, 2008
Stone pigments and Arabic gum on
handmade Sanganer paper
25.4 x 50.8 cm | 10 x 20 in
(OF0804)

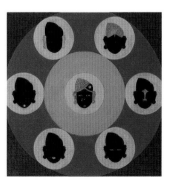

Becoming Krishna, 2009
Stone pigments and Arabic gum on
handmade Sanganer paper
48.3 x 48.3 cm | 19 x 19 in
(OF0903)

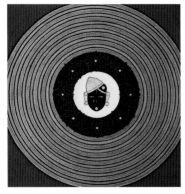

Seven Oceans, Seven Continents, 2010
Stone pigments, Arabic gum and gold
leaf on handmade Sanganer paper
48.3 x 48.3 cm | 19 x 19 in
(OF1001)

Krishna I, 2010
Stone pigments and Arabic gum on
handmade Sanganer paper
76.2 x 46.9 cm | 30 x 18 1/2 in
(OF1005)

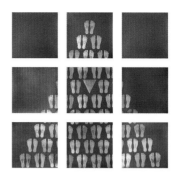

Pilgrimage, 2011
Stone pigments, Arabic gum and gold leaf
on handmade Sanganer paper
75 x 75cm | 29 1/2 x 29 1/2 in (each)
223.5 x 223.5 cm | 88 x 88 in (overall)
(OF1101)

Mt Govardhan, 2010
Stone pigments and Arabic gum on
handmade Sanganer paper
86.4 x 86.4 cm | 34 x 34 in
(OF1002)

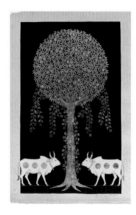

Krishna II, 2010
Stone pigments, Arabic gum and gold
leaf on handmade Sanganer paper
76.2 x 46.9 cm | 30 x 18 1/2 in
(OF1006)

Cosmic Body, 2010
Stone pigments and Arabic gum on
handmade Sanganer paper
48.3 x 25.4 cm | 19 x 10 in
(OF1113)

Mount Meru (Triptych), 2010
Stone pigments, Arabic gum and gold leaf on
handmade Sanganer paper
48.3 x 48.3 cm | 19 x 19 in (each)
48.3 x 114.9 cm | 19 x 45 1/4 in (overall)
(OF1003)

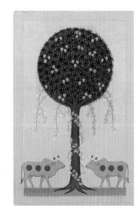

Krishna III, 2010
Stone pigments and Arabic gum on
handmade Sanganer paper
76.2 x 46.9 cm | 30 x 18 1/2 in
(OF1007)

**You Drew Forth the Sun That Was
Hidden in the Water - Rigveda
10.7, 2011**
Stone pigments, Arabic gum and gold
leaf on handmade Sanganer paper
26.7 x 26.7 cm | 10 1/2 x 10 1/2 in
(OF1102 / 971231 AAB)

Creation, 2011
Stone pigments, Arabic gum and gold
leaf on handmade Sanganer paper
170 x 74 cm | 66 7/8 x 29 1/8 in
(OF1103)

Shiv Shakti (Triptych), 2011
Stone pigments and Arabic gum on
handmade Sanganer paper
63.5 x 63.5 cm | 25 x 25 in (each)
63.5 x 190.5 cm | 25 x 75 in (overall)
(OF1106)

Genesis (Triptych), 2011
Stone pigments and Arabic gum on
handmade Sanganer paper
47 x 141 cm | 18 1/2 x 55 1/2 in
(OF1109)

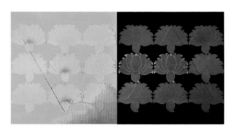

Radha Krishna, 2011
Stone pigments and Arabic gum on
handmade Sanganer paper
63 x 126 cm | 24 3/4 x 49 5/8 in
(OF1104)

The Ladder of the Cosmos, 2011
Stone pigments and Arabic gum on
handmade Sanganer paper
96.5 x 76.2 cm | 38 x 30 in
(OF1107)

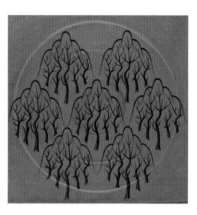

Holy Mountain, 2011
Stone pigments and Arabic gum on
handmade Sanganer paper
63.5 x 63.5 cm | 25 x 25 in
(OF1110)

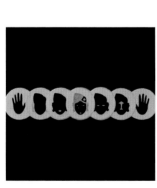

I See Him Now, 2011
Stone pigments and Arabic gum on
handmade Sanganer paper
66 x 66 cm | 26 x 26 in
(OF1105)

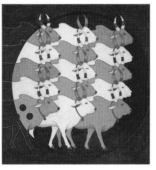

Godhuli Bela, 2011
Stone pigments and Arabic gum on
handmade Sanganer paper
63.5 x 63.5 cm | 25 x 25 in
(OF1108)

**Churning of the Milky Ocean,
2011**
Stone pigments and Arabic gum on
handmade Sanganer paper
38 x 123 cm | 15 x 48 3/8 in
(OF1111)

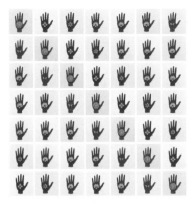

Awakening, 2012
Stone pigments and Arabic gum on
handmade Sanganer paper
24 x 24 cm | 9 1/2 x 9 1/2 in (each)
168 x 168 cm | 66 x 66 in (overall)
(OF1201)

Dawn, 2012
Stone pigments and Arabic gum on
handmade Sanganer paper
63 x 63 cm | 24 3/4 x 24 3/4 in
(OF1202)

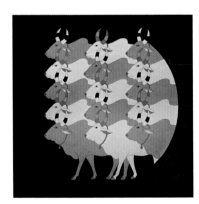

Dusk, 2012
Watercolour on paper
63 x 63 cm | 24 3/4 x 24 3/4 in
(OF1203)

Desert, 2012
Stone pigments and Arabic gum on
handmade Sanganer paper
63 x 63 cm | 24 3/4 x 24 3/4 in
(OF1204)

Essence, 2012
Stone pigments, Arabic gum and gold
leaf on handmade Sanganer paper
25.4 x 81.3 cm | 10 x 32 in
(OF1205)

The Elements, 2012
Watercolour on paper
75 x 19 cm | 29 1/2 x 7 1/2 in
(OF1206)

Dissolution, 2012
Stone pigments, Arabic gum and gold
leaf on handmade Sanganer paper
75 x 19 cm | 29 1/2 x 7 1/2 in
(OF1207)

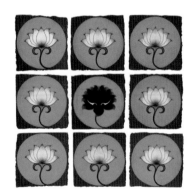

The Blue Lotus, 2012
Stone pigments and Arabic gum on
handmade Sanganer paper
86 x 86 cm | 33 7/8 x 33 7/8 in
(OF1208)

Darshan, 2012
Stone pigments, Arabic gum and gold
leaf on handmade Sanganer paper
25.4 x 50.8 cm | 10 x 20 in
(OF1209)

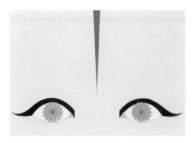

Lotus Eyed, 2013
Stone pigments, Arabic gum and gold
leaf on handmade Sanganer paper
25.4 x 50.8 cm | 10 x 20 in
(OF1303)

Rasa Lila, 2013
Stone pigments and Arabic gum on handmade
Sanganer paper
50.8 x 50.8 cm | 20 x 20 in (each)
101.6 x 101.6 cm. | 40 1/2 x 40 1/2 (overall)
(OF1306)

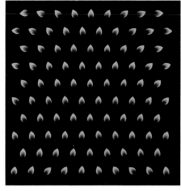

Chakra III, 2013
Stone pigments and Arabic gum on
handmade Sanganer paper
63.5 x 63.5 cm | 25 x 25 in
(OF1309)

Himalaya, 2013
Stone pigments and Arabic gum on
handmade Sanganer paper
68.6 x 68.6 cm | 27 x 27 in
(OF1304)

Chakra I, 2013
Stone pigments and Arabic gum on
handmade Sanganer paper
63.5 x 63.5 cm | 25 x 25 in
(OF1307)

River Raag, 2013
Stone pigments and Arabic gum on
handmade Sanganer paper
66 x 66 cm | 26 x 26 in
(OF1310 / 971142)

1000 Petals, 2013
Stone pigments and Arabic gum on
handmade Sanganer paper
68.6 x 68.6 cm | 27 x 27 in
(OF1305)

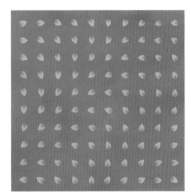

Chakra II, 2013
Stone pigments and Arabic gum on
handmade Sanganer paper
63.5 x 63.5 cm | 25 x 25 in
(OF1308)

Kundalini I, 2014
Stone pigments, Arabic gum and gold
leaf on handmade Sanganer paper
121.9 x 91.4 cm | 48 x 36 in
(OF1401)

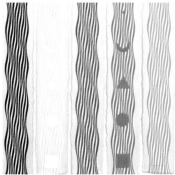

River of Life, 2012
Stone pigments and Arabic gum on
handmade Sanganer paper
96.5 x 96.5 cm | 38 x 38 in
(OF1210)

River of Life, 2014
Stone pigments and Arabic gum on handmade
Sanganer paper
74.9 x 19.1 cm | 29 1/2 x 7 1/2 in (each)
74.9 x 57.3 cm | 29 1/2 x 22 1/2 in (overall)
(OF1403)

Darshan II, 2015
Stone pigments, Arabic gum and gold
leaf on handmade Sanganer paper
68.5 x 68.5 cm | 27 x 27 in
(OF1501)

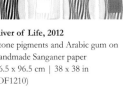

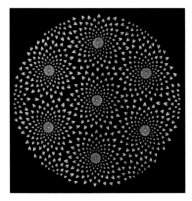

Sun, 2013
Stone pigments, Arabic gum and gold
leaf on handmade Sanganer paper
68.6 x 68.6 cm | 27 x 27 in
(OF1301 / 971387)

Yantra, 2014
Stone pigments and Arabic gum on
handmade Sanganer paper
66 x 66 cm | 26 x 26 in
(OF1404)

One Breath, 2015
Stone pigments and Arabic gum on
handmade Sanganer paper
26.7 x 100.3 cm | 10 1/2 x 39 1/2 in
(OF1502)

Moon, 2013
Stone pigments, Arabic gum and gold
leaf on handmade Sanganer paper
68.6 x 68.6 cm | 27 x 27 in
(OF1302 / 971376)

Kundalini II, 2014
Stone pigments, Arabic gum and gold
leaf on handmade Sanganer paper
121.9 x 91.4 cm | 48 x 36 in
(OF1449)

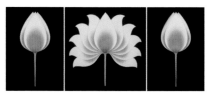

Breath, 2015
Stone pigments and Arabic gum on
handmade Sanganer paper
53.5 x 105.5 cm | 21 1/8 x 41 1/2 in
(OF1503 / 971997 A)

Darshan, 2015
Stone pigments, Arabic gum and gold
leaf on handmade Sanganer paper
63.5 x 63.5 cm | 25 x 25 in
(OF1504 / 971982 A)

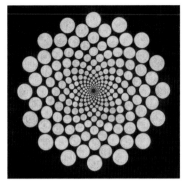

Churning II, 2015
Stone pigments and Arabic gum on
handmade Sanganer paper
91.4 x 91.4 cm | 36 x 36 in
(OF1507)

Breath, 2015
Watercolour on paper
Consists of 7 individual panels, each
measuring:
63.5 x 91.4 cm | 25 x 36 in
72.3 x 91.4 cm | 28.5 x 36 in
81 x 91.4 cm | 32 x 36 in
91.4 x 91.4 cm | 36 x 36 in
81 x 91.4 cm. | 32 x 36 in
72.3 x 91.4 cm | 28.5 x 36 in
63.5 x 91.4 cm | 25 x 36 in
(OF1510)

Blue Himalaya, 2015
Stone pigments and Arabic gum on
handmade Sanganer paper
68.6 x 68.6 cm | 27 x 27 in
(OF1505)

1000 Petals (Blue), 2015
Stone pigments and Arabic gum on
handmade Sanganer paper
91.4 x 91.4 cm | 36 x 36 in
(OF1508)

Breathe, 2015
Watercolour on paper
91.4 x 91.4 cm | 36 x 36 in
(OF1511)

Churning I, 2015
Stone pigments and Arabic gum on
handmade Sanganer paper
91.4 x 91.4 cm | 36 x 36 in
(OF1506)

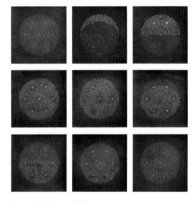

I am the Moon, 2015
Stone pigments, Arabic gum and gold leaf on
handmade Sanganer paper
Consists of 9 individual panels each measuring
35.5 x 35.5 cm | 14 x 14 in (each)
106.5 x 106.5 cm | 42 x 42 in (overall)
(OF1509)

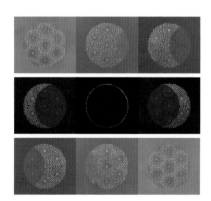

You are the Sun, 2015
Stone pigments, Arabic gum and gold
leaf on handmade Sanganer paper
Consists of 9 individual panels
35.5 x 35.5 cm | 14 x 14 in (each)
35.5 x 320 cm | 14 x 126 in (overall)
(OF1512)

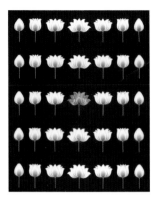

Prana, 2015
Watercolour on paper
(OF1513)

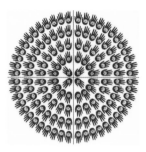

Chakra, 2015
Stone pigments, Arabic gum and gold
leaf on handmade Sanganer paper
91.4 x 91.4 cm | 36 x 36 in (each)
182 x 182 cm | 72 x 72 in (overall)
(OF1519)

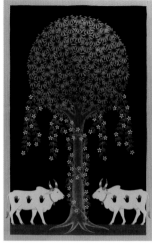

Krishna, 2015
Stone pigments and Arabic gum on
handmade Sanganer paper
76.2 x 46.9 cm | 30 x 18 1/2 in
(OF1522)

Red Himalaya, 2015
Stone pigments and Arabic gum on
handmade Sanganer paper
68.5 x 68.5 cm | 27 x 27 in
(OF1516)

Chakras, 2015
Stone pigments, Arabic gum and gold
leaf on handmade Sanganer paper
61 x 15.2 cm | 24 x 6 in
(OF1520)

Pause , 2015
Stone pigments and Arabic gum on
handmade Sanganer paper
81.3 x 81.3 cm | 32 x 32 in
(OF1523)

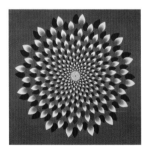

1000 Petals (Red), 2015
Stone pigments and Arabic gum on
handmade Sanganer paper
91.4 x 91.4 cm | 36 x 36 in
(OF1517)

Porous Borders, 2015
Stone pigments, Arabic gum and gold
leaf on handmade Sanganer paper
91.4 x 91.4 cm | 36 x 36 in
(OF1521)

Breath II, 2016
Stone pigments, Arabic gum and gold leaf on
handmade Sanganer paper
Consists of 3 individual panels, each measuring:
64.7 x 91.4 cm | 25.5x 36 in
91.4 x 91.5 cm | 36 x 36 in
64.7 x 91.4 cm | 25.5 x 36 in
64.7 x 274.2 cm | 25.5 x 108 in (overall)
(OF1601 / 971996)

Lotus Eyes, 2016
Stone pigments, Arabic gum and gold
leaf on handmade Sanganer paper
55.8 x 111.7 cm | 22 x 44 in
(OF1602 / 971990)

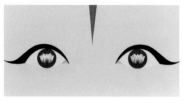

Lotus Eyes, 2016
Stone pigments, Arabic gum and gold
leaf on handmade Sanganer paper
55.8 x 111.7 cm | 22 x 44 in
(OF1608)

Pause II, 2016
Stone pigments and Arabic gum on
handmade Sanganer paper
71.1 x 91.4 cm | 28 x 36 in
(OF1604)

Breathe, 2016
Stone pigments and Arabic gum on
handmade Sanganer paper
91.4 x 91.4 cm | 36 x 36 in
(OF1605)

Breath, 2016
Stone pigments and Arabic gum on handmade
Sanganer paper
Consists of 3 individual panels, each measuring:
64.7 x 91.4 cm | 25.5x 36 in
91.4 x 91.5 cm | 36 x 36 in
64.7 x 91.4 cm | 25.5 x 36 in
64.7 x 274.2 cm | 25.5 x 108 in (overall)
(OF1606)

Kalachakra, 2016
Stone pigments and Arabic gum on
handmade Sanganer paper
27.9 x 27.9 cm | 11 x 11 in (each)
27.9 x 83.8 cm | 11 x 33 in (overall)
(OF1607)

White Star, 2017
Stone pigments and Arabic gum on
handmade Sanganer paper
91.5 x 91.5 cm | 36 1/8 x 36 1/8 in
(OF1701 / 972030)

Breathe II, 2017
Stone pigments, Arabic gum and gold
leaf on handmade Sanganer paper
91.5 x 91.5 cm | 36 1/8 x 36 1/8 in
(OF1702 / 971995)

Chakras, 2017
Stone pigments, Arabic gum and gold
leaf on handmade Sanganer paper
66 x 16.5 cm | 26 x 6 1/2 in
(OF1703 / 971994)

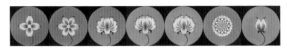

The Golden Lotus, 2017
Stone pigments, Arabic gum and gold
leaf on handmade Sanganer paper
91.5 x 91.5 cm | 36 x 36 in (each)
91.5 x 640 cm | 36 x 252 in (overall)
(OF1704)

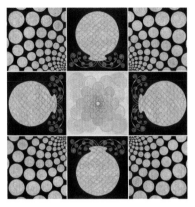

Jambudvipa, 2017
Stone pigments, Arabic gum and gold
leaf on handmade Sanganer paper
27.9 x 27.9 cm | 11 x 11 in (each)
91.5 x 91.5 cm | 36 x 36 in (overall)
(OF1707)

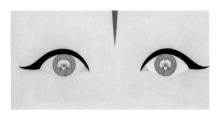

Darshan I, 2018
Stone pigments, Arabic gum and gold
leaf on handmade Sanganer paper
27.9 x 55.9 cm | 11 x 22 in
(OF1801 / 972231 AA)

Black Star, 2017
Stone pigments and Arabic gum on
handmade Sanganer paper
91.5 x 91.5 cm | 36 1/8 x 36 1/8 in
(OF1705)

Lotus, 2017
Stone pigments and Arabic gum on
handmade Sanganer paper
91.4 x 73.7 cm | 36 x 29 in
(OF1708)

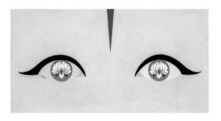

Darshan II, 2018
Stone pigments, Arabic gum and gold leaf on
handmade Sanganer paper
27.9 x 55.9 cm | 11 x 22 in
(OF1802)

Sthalapadma, 2017
Stone pigments and Arabic gum on
handmade Sanganer paper
58.4 x 58.4 cm | 23 x 23 in (each)
175.3 x 175.3 cm | 69 x 69 in (overall)
(OF1706)

Lotus Eyes, 2017
Stone pigments and Arabic gum on
handmade Sanganer paper
55.8 x 111.7 cm | 22 x 44 in
(OF1709)

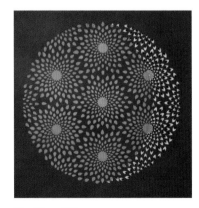

New Moon, 2018
Stone pigments, Arabic gum and gold
leaf on handmade Sanganer paper
91.4 x 91.4 cm | 36 x 36 in
(OF1803 / 972260)

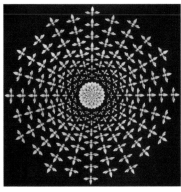

Scent of The Lotus II, 2018
Stone pigments, Arabic gum and gold
leaf on handmade Sanganer paper
81.3 x 81.3 cm | 32 x 32 in
(OF1804 / 972231 A)

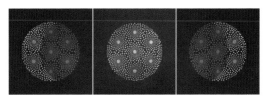

Moon (Triptych), 2017-2018
Stone pigments and Arabic gum on
handmade Sanganer paper
91.4 x 91.4 cm | 36 x 36 in (each)
91.4 x 274.3 cm | 36 x 108 in (overall)
(OF1807 / 972231 B)

Scent of the Lotus III, 2018
Stone pigments, Arabic gum and gold
leaf on handmade Sanganer paper
91.4 x 91.4 cm | 36 x 36 in
(OF1810)

Scent of the Lotus I, 2018
Stone pigments and Arabic gum on
handmade Sanganer paper
81.3 x 81.3 cm | 32 x 32 in
(OF1805 / 972220)

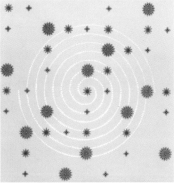

Constellation, 2018
Stone pigments and Arabic gum on
handmade Sanganer paper
91.4 x 91.4 cm | 36 x 36 in
(OF1808)

Metamorphosis I, 2018
Stone pigments, Arabic gum and gold leaf
on handmade Sanganer paper
Consists of 5 panels
27.9 x 27.9 cm each | 11 x 11 in (each)
27.9 x 139.5 cm | 11 x 55 in (overall)
(OF1814)

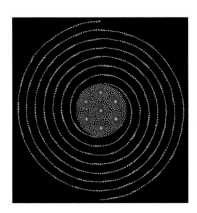

Creation, 2018
Stone pigments, Arabic gum and gold
leaf on handmade Sanganer paper
91.4 x 91.4 cm | 36 x 36 in
(OF1806 / 972216)

Lotus Eyes, 2018
Stone pigments and Arabic gum on
handmade Sanganer paper
30.5 x 57.1 cm | 12 x 22 1/2 in
(OF1809)

Scent of the Lotus IV, 2018
Stone pigments and Arabic gum on
handmade Sanganer paper
91.4 x 91.4 cm | 36 x 36 in
(OF1811)

Metamorphosis II, 2018
Stone pigments, Arabic gum and gold
leaf on handmade Sanganer paper
Consists of 5 panels
27.9 x 27.9 cm | 11 x 11 in (each)
27.9 x 139.5 cm | 11 x 55 in (overall)
(OF1815)

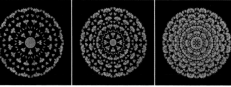

Bhramari (Triptych), 2019
Stone pigments, Arabic gum and gold
leaf on handmade Sanganer paper
Consists of 3 panels
91.4 x 91.4 cm | 36 x 36 in (each)
91.4 x 274 cm | 36 x 108 in (overall)
(OF1901)

Neelkamal, 2019
Stone pigments and Arabic gum on
handmade Sanganer paper
58.4 x 58.4 cm | 23 x 23 in (each)
58.4 x 292 cm | 23 x 115 in (overall)
(OF1903)

Scent of the Lotus V, 2018
Stone pigments and Arabic gum on
handmade Sanganer paper
91.4 x 91.4 cm | 36 x 36 in
(OF1812)

Breath III, 2019
Stone pigments, Arabic gum on handmade
Sanganer paper
Consists of 3 panels:
91.4 x 60.9 cm | 36 x 24 in
91.4 x 91.4 cm | 36 x 36 in
91.4 x 60.9 cm | 36 x 24 in
(OF1904)

Kama (Diptych), 2019
Stone pigments, Arabic gum and gold leaf on
handmade Sanganer paper
63.5 x 127 cm | 25 x 50 in (each)
63.5 x 254 cm | 25 x 100 in (overall)
(OF1902)

Darshan IV, 2019
Stone pigments, Arabic gum and gold
leaf on handmade Sanganer paper
27.9 x 55.9 cm | 11 x 22 in
(OF1906)

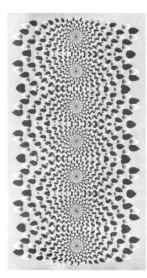

The Seven Chakras, 2019
Stone pigments and Arabic gum on handmade
Sanganer paper
116.8 x 66 cm | 46 x 26 in
(OF1905)

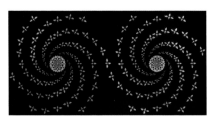

Brahmri, 2018
Stone pigments, Arabic gum and gold
leaf on handmade Sanganer paper
76.2 x 147.3 cm | 30 x 58 in
(OF1813)

Darshan III, 2019
Stone pigments, Arabic gum and gold
leaf on handmade Sanganer paper
27.9 x 55.9 cm | 11 x 22 in
(OF1907)

Acknowledgements

I would like to thank Faith & John Singh and Frances Ronaldson for their support in setting me off on this journey; Ajay Sharma and Desmond Lazaro for generously teaching me and showing me the way; Chitterman Kumawat – both guru and assistant – and particularly Jagdish Sharma for his incredible artistic assistance over the last few years. I'd also like to thank my gallerists: Conor Macklin, Kajoli Khanna and Charles Moore at the Grosvenor Gallery, Peter Nagy and Aparajita Jain at Nature Morte and Sundaram Tagore from the Sundaram Tagore Gallery. And of course, I'd like to thank my family, Ibby, Sam and Adam, and most of all, Willie, for all their encouragement, love and belief.

First published in India in 2019 by
HarperCollins *Publishers* India
A-75, Sector 57, Noida, Uttar Pradesh 201301, India
www.harpercollins.co.in

2 4 6 8 10 9 7 5 3 1
Copyright © Olivia Fraser 2019
Artworks © Olivia Fraser 2019
Copyright for the individual pieces vests with their respective authors

P-ISBN: 978-93-5357-394-2
E-ISBN: 978-93-5357-395-9

Typeset in Garamond Premier Pro by 11.5/16

Designed by *Bonita Vaz-Shimray*
Edited by *Karan Singh*

Printed and bound at
Thomson Press (India) Ltd.